GENDER EQUALITY

at Work

First published in 2019.

ISBN: 978-1-86922-802-6
eISBN: 978-1-86922-803-3 (ePDF)

Published by KR Publishing
P O Box 3954
Randburg 2125
Republic of South Africa

Tel: (011) 706-6009
Fax: (011) 706-1127
E-mail: orders@knowres.co.za Website: www.kr.co.za

Layout and design: Cia Joubert, cia@knowres.co.za
Cover design: Marlene de'Lorme, marlene@knowres.co.za
Editing & proofreading: Valda Strauss: valda@global.co.za
Project management: Cia Joubert, cia@knowres.co.za
Index created with TExtract/www.Texyz.com

GENDER EQUALITY
at Work

Some are more equal than others

Dr Nitasha Ramparsad

kr
publishing

2019

Contents

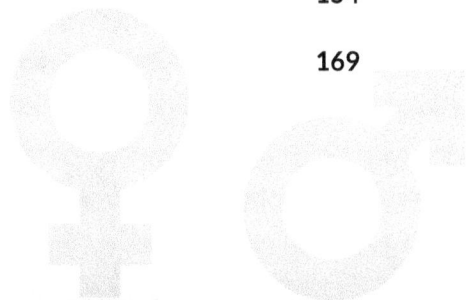

About the Author

Dr Nitasha Ramparsad holds a PhD in Political Science from the University of the Witwatersrand. Her study focused on the role of the Department of Public Service and Administration in the fulfilment of its commitments to gender equality through the rollout of gender mainstreaming as a strategy for gender equality. She is the Director for Leadership Support at the National School of Government and is committed to the empowerment of both men and women in the ongoing leadership challenges faced by the African continent. Her interest lies in social justice research and the pursuit of gender equality. She has published extensively in international peer-reviewed journals and most recently presented at the South African Project Management Summit, in February 2019. Nitasha is committed to developing the African continent and producing knowledge unique to the African diaspora.

Nitasha was nominated for the Gender Mainstreaming Awards 2019 in the category Positive Role Model and has been featured in a publication called *Purposeful Woman* inspiring high school girls. She was also featured in the *We Will Lead Africa* journal, Volume 2 with a specific focus on Women in Governance.

Acknowledgements

I would like to acknowledge the support of my husband, Vikash Ramparsad, and my mother, Jeannie Moodly, for their unwavering support in the completion of this book. One's mother's lessons are so important in guiding one's life and I am truly grateful to have you as mine. I would like to thank my son Rohan who pushes me to be the best version of myself. I would also like to acknowledge the giver of life, my Lord and Saviour, Jesus Christ, who has blessed me beyond measure. I would like to finally acknowledge Knowledge Resources for their belief in my vision and their commitment to gender equality on the continent. Specific thanks to Cia Joubert, Zia Attlee and Wilhelm Crous for your patience and guidance in the development of this book.

Preface

Gender Equality at Work: Some are more equal than others emanated from my own experience as a State official where efforts around the use of gender mainstreaming as a strategy for gender equality could not yield the desired results. The lessons that have emerged from this experience can be applied to all sectors as the barriers to gender equality remain the same for Human Resource practitioners regardless of the arena in which they practice. The book aims to provide practical guidance on how to circumvent the many barriers facing the implementation of gender mainstreaming as a strategy for gender quality. It puts forward that an enabling environment must be created in order for any initiatives around gender equality to be achieved and suggests tools and strategies to ensure that the overall goal of gender equality in the workplace is met.

Book Outline

Chapter 1: Not another feminist rant!

The current status quo of women in South Africa is discussed with a brief history of the last 10 years' progress towards gender equality. The struggles facing women in the workplace are discussed and a the case for the use of gender mainstreaming as a strategy for gender equality is made. A holistic approach is proposed with a focus on leadership at all levels.

Chapter 2: Operationalising gender equality

Key concepts and legislation are explained with relevance for Human Resource practitioners. The global context is provided and then is brought to the South African context with a specific focus on how to use Gender Mainstreaming to move beyond compliance measures.

Chapter 3: What Works? Reflecting on Cases for Gender Mainstreaming

An overview of country and private sector cases that are viewed as forerunners in the gender equality struggle are showcased. The Chapter nine institutions are discussed briefly and serve as a resource to Human Resource practitioners across sectors.

Chapter 4: Developing Senior Management Buy-In

The important role senior management plays in creating an enabling environment is explored and practical guidance on holding senior management accountable is offered. In addition, the role of leadership in the African context is provided, with anecdotes from key leaders facing challenges in the workplace.

Chapter 5: Nurturing a supportive community

Collaborations are an important part of developing an enabling environment. Organisations are encouraged to seek out relevant and significant partners in the South African gender landscape to assist and support their organisations in the development of a workplace that favours gender equality. Specific success cases are discussed under the auspices of the Commission for Gender Equality. The development of Gender Action Plans and their relevance as implementation tools is presented.

Chapter 6: Setting the rules

Policy development is discussed with specific reference to the development of sexual harassment. Policy is a necessary step in the mainstreaming efforts towards gender equality in the workplace. The development of policy and practical guidance is offered with reference to the over-arching policies on gender equality in the country.

Chapter 7: Holding up a mirror

Monitoring and evaluation mechanisms with suggested criteria are provided for Human Resource practitioners as well as links with practical information on how to link policy to the necessary skills required for the implementation of gender mainstreaming as a strategy for gender equality.

Chapter 8: Longevity

The use of case study development is explained with reference to how to develop cases to capture lessons. The value of the worst case is discussed for its importance in learning in the workplace. The case studies will form onboard resources for Human Resource practitioners developed and driven by themselves as lessons that can be referred to in the longevity of the organisation.

Chapter 9: Sustainable Campaigns

The value of constant messaging and sustainable gender campaigns is explored. The notion of campaigns is explored in the physical and digital space. These initiatives are highlighted for their value in driving the goals of the Gender Action Plans that will be developed for the entire organisation.

Chapter 10: Where to now?

This closing chapter suggests areas for future collaborations and possible practical projects to be considered by Human Resource practitioners.

This book therefore offers practical guidance to Human Resource practitioners on how to use gender mainstreaming as a strategy to address gender equality in the workplace. Notably, the book also offers some theoretical guidance on understanding gender mainstreaming concepts and their application in the workplace. It is imperative for Human Resource practitioners to consider the use of the tools suggested in this book to move towards a workplace that values gender equality beyond compliance measures and events management.

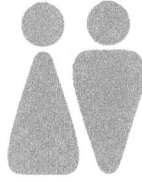

CHAPTER 1

Not another feminist rant!

Almost 50 percent of men think that it is sufficient when just one in ten senior leaders in their company is a woman. One-third of women agree.[1]

Gender bias is attracting new interest with the #MeToo and #TimesUp movements. These movements have been raising awareness around gender inequality and sexual harassment around the globe. In my experience efforts addressing gender equality are limited to Women's Month and the 16 Days of Activism for No Violence Against Women and Children in the South African context. Whilst these efforts are commendable, a much more sustainable approach must be explored that goes beyond what I deem, events management. The Women's March of 1956 is always used as the main theme to celebrate the activism of women; however, it is imperative to assess how far we have come since then. The Global Talent Competitiveness Index ranks South Africa as 66 in the gender earnings gap yet also ranks women as 86 in terms of leadership opportunities afforded to them. There seems to be no correlation between efforts afforded to positioning women and closing the gender earnings gap.[2] According to the World Economic Forum, South Africa is ranked 17th out of 136 countries, which has largely been attributed to the efforts assigned to "Women's Month" as opposed to other countries who only celebrate "Women's Day". More women and girls in South Africa have access to education and paid jobs, yet patriarchal attitudes continue to stifle the position of women. Progressive laws can only go so far in addressing injustices.

I have been in the South African training and development space, both in the public and private sectors, for the past 15 years and have come to the realisation that where gender equality is concerned, capacity building is often punted as a quick fix. This is but one piece of a larger proverbial pie. In order to provide sustained efforts towards the ultimate goal of gender equality in the workplace a more holistic approach must be employed. I found common themes with the barriers to gender equality in organisations across sectors, lack of support from senior management, poor resource allocation and an overall poor environment for the embodiment of gender equality in the workplace. Human Resource practitioners are in need of a resource that can assist in ultimately working towards sustainable and practical solutions. This book challenges Human Resource practitioners to consider the use of gender mainstreaming as a strategy for gender equality and ultimately provides guidelines for practical measures that can be taken to institute sustainable interventions towards gender equality in the workplace.

According to the Midyear Population Statistics of 2017, women make up half of South Africa's population, yet they remain largely under-represented in positions of authority and power. If you consider the entire workforce, 44 in every 100 employed individuals are women, according to labour data released for the second quarter of 2017[3]. Women fill 44% of skilled posts, which includes managers, professionals and technicians. This figure hasn't shifted much over the years; it was 44% in September 2002. Although South Africa has made great strides, gender representivity is still below the 50% mark for positions that come with a great deal of influence, according to data from 2014. Women comprised 32% of Supreme Court of Appeal judges, 31% of advocates, 30% of ambassadors and 24% of heads of state-owned enterprises. If we take a brief look at the Top 40 JSE listed companies, only one company had a female CEO. Parliament fares a lot better. South Africa is ranked as the tenth country in the world with the most number of females in parliament, according to the Inter-Parliamentary Union, with just over 4 in every 10 benches held by a women. In 2016, 107 of the sitting mayors (or 39%) were female, slightly lower than the 42% recorded in 2017. Municipalities in Limpopo led the charge in gender equality, followed by North West and Eastern Cape. Today, only 5% of S&P 500 companies are led by women, according to Catalyst, a non-profit CEO watchdog. That figure is all the more remarkable when one considers that 73% of global firms allegedly have equal-opportunity policies in place, according to a survey by the International Labour Organization (ILO).

The McKinsey & Company Report of 2016 reveals the subordinate position of women on the African continent. The data tallied from over 200 African companies and interviews with 35 women leaders reflects the regional dynamics in gender diversity in leadership on the continent. McKinsey & Company found that companies with more gender-diverse boards tend to perform better financially – earnings before interest and taxes (EBIT) margin of top quartile companies in terms of gender diversity is 20% higher than the industry average. However, women in senior management still face many challenges when placed in a senior management role.

The report advised that amongst the obstacles faced by women, the following were highlighted as the major barriers for women in senior management:

★　Gender issues are not taken seriously enough – in Africa, only one in three CEOs has gender diversity on his or her agenda.

★　The barriers women face in the workplace are poorly understood – organisations do not share women leaders' views of the impediments to their success.

★　Programmes to redress the gender balance do not tackle the right issues – lack of understanding of the reasons for women's under-representation means efforts to tackle it can miss their target.

Women in South Africa who had participated in the study noted that they used many personal strategies to circumvent the barriers experienced at a senior management level. They claimed that a robust work ethic; persistence in achieving goals and willingness to take risks; resilience in the face of adversity; commitment to professional development; proactively seeking career opportunities and ways to improve as a professional; and having mentors, sponsors and peer networks assisted them in facing their challenges. Interestingly, the challenge at a personal level of the private/public space balance was not included but it can be assumed that women need networks and communities to support their private lives whilst undertaking their leadership roles in the public space. This book also looks at the mechanisms that are needed to support women's unpaid labour in the private space through policies in the workplace.

A cursory inspection of current programmes/interventions for transformation specifically aimed at gender equality reveal that these tend to be too academic in focus and do not offer enough practical guidance to practitioners as to the "how to" aspects. A big focus is placed on training individuals with little or no mechanisms being present within the workplace to enable change. Despite the practical nature of this book, it is an also an attempt to reflect on a common understanding of gender mainstreaming as a strategy for gender equality. It is absolutely critical that organisations address the major issue of gender equality to ensure a more successful and equal space for South Africans. This can only be led by progressive leadership at all levels but what does this mean and how is this different from management? The role of senior management leadership is explored as a critical factor in implementing gender mainstreaming as a strategy for gender equality but again, leadership at all levels is advocated as the main driver of success.

Many organisations that subscribe to gender equality outperform those who do not. Before you are able to approach a gender equality strategy, you must reflect on the following questions[4]:

★ What would our organisation look like if our gender equality goals were met?

★ What are we missing out on by not maximising the talents of both genders?

★ What do we see that tells us we have room to improve our gender equality?

★ What are examples of times we have gotten gender equality right?

In order to take this forward, a new way of thinking must be inculcated in senior management. Gender mainstreaming can only be effective as a strategy towards gender equality if the senior management takes accountability for the implementation thereof. Employees at all levels must take responsibility for upholding gender equality as a core value; however, this must be concretised in the policies, culture and operations of an organisation. From a leadership perspective, organisational values are seen as the underlying attitudes and beliefs that help determine individual behaviour of both personnel and leaders. I am advocating that for an area such as gender equality, Human

Resource practitioners must provide the tools and skills for managers to become leaders and for employees to inculcate gender mainstreaming as an operational strategy aimed at transformation in the workplace.

According to the McKinsey 2018 *Women in the Workplace* Report, at the current rate of progress, the global gender gap will take 100 years to close, compared to 83 last year. The two biggest drivers of representation are hiring and promotions, and companies are disadvantaging women in these areas from the beginning. Although women earn more bachelor's degrees than men, and have for decades, they are less likely to be hired into entry-level jobs. At the first critical step up to manager, the disparity widens further. Women are less likely to be hired into manager-level jobs, and they are far less likely to be promoted into them – for every one hundred men promoted to manager, seventy-nine women are. Largely because of these gender gaps, men end up holding 62% of manager positions, while women hold only 38%.

These stats should serve as a red flag, as the hiring and promotion of women has a profound effect on how this picture will look as women continue up the pipeline.

Example: Performance bias helps explain early gaps in hiring and promotions

Research shows that we tend to overestimate men's performance and underestimate women's. As a result, men are often hired and promoted based on their potential, while women are often hired and promoted based on their track record. This may be particularly acute for women at the start of their careers, when their track records are relatively short.[5]

This book is an attempt to provide you as a Human Resource practitioner or as someone seeking transformation, to seek the use of gender mainstreaming as a strategy for gender equality. This term exists in pockets and is often misunderstood. The book dispels the myths around gender mainstreaming as a strategy and highlights the success of using this as a major initiative in operationalising a transformation strategy aimed at the ultimate goal of gender equality.

Gender equality is approached as a stand-alone project and is often confused with diversity management. Whilst this is an element of diversity management, gender equality is an issue on its own and must be seen as a part of diversity. In addition, marginalised issues such as disability and race must also be considered for cross-pollination. However, the scope of this book focuses on gender equality with some links being offered to assess disability and race in Chapters 8 and 9.

Gender is one aspect of the diversity debate and must be treated as part of an overall transformation strategy that will encompass elements of race and class in order for a holistic strategy to be developed. Equality refers to fairness, and in particular to universal access (to employment or health care (for instance), whereas diversity is about recognising and embracing differences within an institution, workforce or society. In this respect, the two concepts are somewhat at odds with each other, with one stressing homogeneity (sameness) and the other highlighting heterogeneity (difference). Even so, equality and diversity are very often used together, sometimes even interchangeably.

Often, people will speak of ensuring equality by recognising diversity. While this may seem a contradiction at first, the ethnic, religious and sexual diversity of contemporary societies demands such a holistic approach. In order to treat individuals with equal respect, care and attention, their diverse individual needs must be taken into account.

Those people who strive for diversity in organisations emphasise the value of difference. A diverse workforce, for instance, will be much better equipped to meet the needs of their diverse customers or clients. Furthermore, the more valued each member of a workforce feels, the more productive they are likely to be.

Ethnicity (or race), religion and sexuality are not the only factors to consider. Societies are also divided into groups of varying wealth (or class), age, physical ability or mental health and of course gender. While equality is often backed by anti-discrimination laws, in practice, it requires an ongoing commitment to diversity.[6]

This book stresses the need for equal access for men and women in the workplace, meaning that women and men must be provided with the correct capacity in terms of skills, human and financial resources to achieve their goals and be afforded the same opportunities and experiences. This, I advocate, can be regulated through policies for equality rather than equity. The terms 'equity' and 'equality' are sometimes used interchangeably, which can lead to confusion because while these concepts are related, there are also important distinctions between them.

Equity, as we have seen, involves trying to understand and give people what they need to enjoy full, healthy lives. Equality, in contrast, aims to ensure that everyone gets the same things in order to enjoy full, healthy lives. Like equity, equality aims to promote fairness and justice, but it can only work if everyone starts from the same place and needs the same things. I believe this to be true for both men and women; single working mothers and single working fathers should be offered the same benefits. The same benefits should apply for maternity and paternity policies and men and women's work should be valued equally.

Example[7]:

The same distinction between equity and equality can be seen when it comes to health and care. For example, Canada's publicly-funded health care system is based on the concept of equality. It is designed to ensure that everyone has the same access to health care providers and services regardless of their ability to pay for care. Again, this seems fair. But it only goes so far in promoting justice because it ignores other factors – such as language, place of residence, sexual orientation and gender – that can also act as barriers to care.

Similarly, in the workplace, barriers for access must be addressed with practical interventions to ensure equality.

Equality in the workplace is never a cut-and-dried process. This requires commitment from both management and the Human Resources Department. Essentially, equality in the workplace means that no person should experience or fear discrimination based on their gender, sex, age, race, etc. The laws are designed to open the door for complaints. Before anti-discrimination laws, complaining about discrimination in the workplace was only likely to cause further discrimination and even termination without cause. Now, victims are entitled to have their complaints taken seriously.[8] Discrimination can present itself as a form of disparate treatment and a blatant form of discrimination is where someone is treated less favourably because they are a member of a protected class.

Example of Disparate Treatment

Requiring a more difficult hiring test for minorities than others is a direct form of discrimination.

The laws protecting South Africans against discrimination are discussed at length in Chapter 3. Acknowledging laws and actually enforcing equality are two very different concepts.

Example of Discrimination Based on Age

A young tech start-up may discriminate based on age in the hiring process without directly making the process of discrimination apparent. Filing a claim against this type of discrimination is difficult.

There is a major gap in how gender equality is approached in the workplace and this centers on the involvement of men as champions.

Male Champions of Change Initiative

The Male Champions of Change initiative, led by Sex Discrimination Commissioner Elizabeth Broderick, has received widespread support from the Commonwealth Bank and its CEO, Ian Narev. Narev's strong leadership in gender diversity was emphasised at the Commonwealth Bank announcing that the company was in the process of becoming a signatory of the Women's Empowerment Principles. Commitment to the principles helps to elevate the issue of women's representation in leadership, giving it the same treatment as other transformational business objectives.

According to the 2014 report on *Men as Agents of Change* led by the United Nations Development Fund, there was a clear shared consensus on three points:

1. We cannot achieve gender equality without men. Participants cited a number of ways in which men can actively promote gender equality: by taking parental leave, by sharing the double shift of childcare and housework, by challenging their peers and calling out sexist behaviours where they occur – in the street, in the workplace, and online – and by speaking about the ways in which gender inequality limits the opportunities of boys and men also.

2. Men will also benefit from gender equality. Men have a great deal to gain from gender equality. Restrictive gender roles and stereotypes harm men as well as women, boys as well as girls. For real change to happen, everybody has to acknowledge and understand that better for women means better for all.

3. Engagement is not easy. Engaging men as change agents for gender equality is not easy. But there are many men who listen, understand, and want to play their part. We must work with men to secure their involvement in making gender equality a reality.

As a Human Resource practitioner, it is important to acknowledge the way in which masculinities are constructed and to try and build a supportive environment for the growth of both sexes. Consider the following anecdote:

Men at Work[9]:

The same social structures that discriminate against women shape our expectations of men and put pressure on men and boys to act in certain ways. Boys quickly learn to suppress behaviours and emotions that are associated with femininity. Restrictive gender stereotypes and representations can contribute to educational underachievement in boys, higher suicide rates in men and a lack of encouragement for men that want to work with children or in nursing. The same narrow definitions that lead to girls growing up believing that careers in science, technology and maths are not suitable choices for them, mean that boys are unlikely to think of careers in caring professions. The same stereotypes that

---

suggest ambitious and powerful women are aggressive and unfeminine mean that boys learn quickly that they must not show weakness or vulnerability; boys don't cry. Research has demonstrated that men who work in male-dominated industries such as heavy industry frequently suffer increased health problems or become socially isolated when they retire. Therefore, many men will have much to gain through gender equality that allows for new ways of working and living for both men and women.

The Hays Gender Diversity Report 2017

This report puts forward the benefits of gender equality in the workplace. According to the report which focuses on five key areas in the workplace – ambition, self-promotion, equal pay, career opportunities and gender diversity policies – having a gender diversity policy in place has a positive effect on both men and women.[10]

Encourages female ambition

As shown in the report, 50% of women and 70% of men aspire to reach a top leadership position in their career. However, the number of women reaching these leadership positions is remarkably low. Having a gender diversity policy in place will help to encourage women to continue to develop in their careers, helping to create a sustainable pipeline for talented women when moving into senior roles.

Allows a focus on employee self-promotion

The report showed that many men and women do not feel that they have the opportunity to self-promote in the workplace. With gender diversity policies in place, such as mentoring and networking, this allows a platform for workers to communicate and voice their ambitions. This will not only make workers feel they can progress but it will also increase career motivation and satisfaction.

It'll help to narrow the gender divide

Although the gender divide is still prevalent in the workplace, it is narrowing, albeit slowly. Organisations that position gender diversity as a business necessity are bringing more awareness to diversity issues and are helping to tackle problems that would otherwise remain stagnant. This ensures that companies are progressing and moving forward their diversity, helping to create a more equal workforce.

Men and women both feel the benefits of gender diversity policies

The existence of gender diversity policies has a positive impact on both men and women as findings from the report show that respondents working for a company with a gender diversity policy in place are more likely to think there is equal pay between genders. What's more, as a more diverse organisation is likely to generate better results than a less diverse one, it is men and women who will reap the rewards. Again, this will motivate workers and increase satisfaction in their careers.

Gender diversity is an ongoing issue that many workplaces are looking to solve. Most organisations can fail to recognise the impact of a gender-diverse workplace and instead concentrate on other initiatives. As these five benefits show, not only does a gender diversity policy increase positivity in the workplace but it also helps to create a more gender-balanced workforce

Hays's research echoes the sentiments of this book's focus: transformation in the workplace will encourage, above all, a more productive and profitable workplace.

In this book, I focus on:

1. The importance of understanding gender mainstreaming as a strategy towards gender equality. The concept of collaborations and building a supportive community for the implementation of gender mainstreaming is put forward with an emphasis on identifying key role players that can be a resource for building gender equality in the workplace.

2. The development of key tools such as a Gender Action Plan and specific long- and short-term monitoring and evaluation plans are also explained with an emphasis on the role of senior management leadership, but highlighting the need for gender mainstreaming to become the responsibility of all employees at an organisation by proposing leadership at all levels.

In order to look at gender equality, you must assess your organisation in terms of how it values equality and diversity. I advocate for taking certain measures at the outset. You cannot attempt a transformation strategy in an environment that does not foster or support change. What is the situation in your organisation? How are the various job categories at your workplace divided between men and women? Are some already reasonably balanced? Are leadership positions as a category more skewed than others? How does your organisation compare to its competitors in the same industry or sector? If you're going to try to fix a problem, you must first be able to describe it. You have to know what the numbers were yesterday if you want to change them today.[11]

The mainstreaming of gender as a strategy for gender equality is however not limited to a numbers game. You will need to assess the status of current policies and projects in how they approach gender equality. For example, how are the concerns of women taken into account when rolling out the core business of your organisation? How well do people accept and respect women as chairs of meetings? How many women are allotted for accountable positions and positions of leadership (this does not always equate to just senior management but could be key roles such as the Director for Finance who reports to the Chief Financial Officer – this role is a key operational role).

In order to achieve gender targets and to improve gender relations as a consequence of the implementation of any project or programme, projects must be planned in such a way that gender issues are taken into account in each and every stage of the project and that gender analysis is used throughout. This is called gender planning. M&E is an important part of the planning process because they monitor the impact of planned activities on the target group and assess whether the targets set by the project are actually met. I advocate that gender mainstreaming must be approached as a top-down led intervention for the ultimate goal of gender equality and that managers must by and large be encouraged to inculcate leadership values into operations. The latter will, in my opinion, lead to the embodiment of leadership at all levels. Reflect on the case study below – the actions of the World Bank are just as relevant today as many of the same barriers to gender mainstreaming still exist.

Case study: The World Bank: gender and monitoring in water and sanitation projects

In 1996, the World Bank created a Toolkit on Water and Sanitation with various instruments suggesting how to best integrate a gender approach in the planning process of water and sanitation. Among these instruments are terms of reference for a gender analysis during monitoring and evaluation. In particular, it is suggested:

★ to produce gender-disaggregated data and gender-sensitive indicators;

★ to measure the impact of the project on women and men separately;

★ to analyse the participation of women and men in projects and their access to resources;

★ to examine the staff attitudes towards gender issues;

★ to assess the training of women and men in areas like maintenance and hygiene education;

★ to examine how much women and men could decide the type of technology used and the siting of facilities;

★ to involve community women and men in data collection and analysis;

★ to organise meetings to inform all stakeholders on monitoring and evaluation findings, including project staff and communities;

★ to identify areas for further research;

★ to analyse additional benefits from the project, if and how they were gained and how they were used;

★ to analyse additional costs in time or labour for men or women generated by the paper;

★ to draw lessons and provide recommendations.[12]

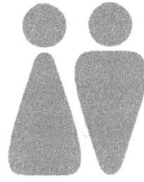

CHAPTER 2

Operationalising gender equality

'If HR isn't committed to gender diversity and isn't championing it, the needle won't move.'

Ursula Mead, InHerSight (Ursula Mead, CEO and founder of InHerSight, a website that allows users to rate how female-friendly companies are)

2018 saw the recognition of maternity leave for both men and women as a major priority. Netflix, Microsoft and other tech giants led the way in offering paid parental leave last year, and more companies have followed suit, including soup maker Campbell's and online purveyor Etsy, which rolled out an astounding 26 weeks of paid time off for new moms and dads earlier this year (2019).[13] More than half of employers also now offer flexible work options such as telecommuting and flexitime, according to the Society for Human Resource Management's 2016 Employee Benefits research report. As a Human Resource practitioner, you need to be positioned in each stage of the employee life cycle in order to regulate and influence change.

> "HR needs to be a part of each step in the employee life cycle."
> Barry Coleman, a former HR manager at The Washington Post Co.

Twenty-five years of democracy in South Africa reveal that organisations across sectors still by and large view gender equality as meeting equity targets. Many organisations feel that they have met their obligations to gender equality by appointing the requisite number of women within their staff compliment. This book reflects that numbers alone are not the answer to gender equality in the workplace. This book is informed by the decade spent rolling out gender mainstreaming and leadership interventions. This experience has proven to be invaluable in informing how I view the barriers to the mainstreaming of gender as a strategy for gender equality. The main criticism of the public service is that it is far too bureaucratic and therefore almost stands in its own way. This book attempts to dispel that myth by revealing that in fact there are many gains being made and lessons to be drawn from the work being done that can be applied across sectors.

I have found that the misconception associated with gender equality is that this theme must be addressed during specific times of the year: International Women's Day, Women's Month and the 16 Days of Activism for No Violence Against Women and Children. Whilst these periods are important they do not adequately address gender equality in the workplace on an everyday basis. The inculcation of gender concerns on an everyday basis repositions this important theme from being an events exercise to one of operational importance. This book offers Human Resource practitioners and those working in transformation practical guidance as to how to go about creating an enabling environment for gender equality in the workplace using gender mainstreaming as a strategy and including men as agents of change.

Let us take a closer look at how gender mainstreaming emerged as a strategy for gender equality. "Gender refers to the economic, social and cultural attributes and opportunities associated with being male or female"[14]. The United Nations Population Fund notes that biological characteristics are associated with societal roles and expectations, but they differ from society to society and evolve over a period. The position of women has changed dramatically since the first formal initiatives towards equality beginning with the South African Women's March in 1954. Gender equity can be described as the process of ensuring fairness and equal distribution of resources among men and women. "Equity leads to equality and where gender inequality exists it is the women who are excluded in relation to decision-making and access to economic and social resources".[15] In the 1970s, it was envisaged that in order to achieve gender equality separate interventions specifically aimed at women were needed. In the run-up to the 1985 UN Decade for Women: Equality, Development and Peace Gathering in Nairobi, it was realised that a more streamlined approach was needed.[16]

By allowing women-specific activities to be separate, efforts at equality were essentially marginalised. It was therefore envisaged that a mainstreaming strategy for gender would assist in embedding gender concerns in all areas and sectors. In 1987, the UN Commission on the Status of Women took the lead role in coordinating and promoting social and economic issues for women's empowerment.

The UN Commission on the Status of Women focused on women's issues as part of the mainstream. (See *A Short History of the Commission on the Status of Women*)[17]. The UN Commission on the Status of Women as the coordinating body then convened a further conference in 1995 where 189 countries were represented and became signatory to the Beijing Platform For Action which advocated that equality for women with men be achieved in law and practice and not as a separate "women's issue".

The Beijing Platform for Action was not, however, conceptualised in a vacuum and stipulated various criteria to ensure the implementation of gender mainstreaming as a strategy for gender equality:

> The General Assembly in Resolution 52/100 (December 1997) requested all bodies within the UN system that deal with programme and budgetary matters to ensure that all programmes, medium-term plans and programme budgets visibly mainstream a gender perspective.[18]

The mainstreaming strategy of the UN Commission on the Status of Women therefore advocates that responsibility for mainstreaming rests at the highest-level echelons of governance and development organisations within the UN to develop an accountability and monitoring system for the mainstreaming of gender, and describes gender mainstreaming as:

> ...the process of assessing the implications for women and men of any planned action, including legislation, policies or programmes, in all areas and at all levels. It is a strategy for making women's as well as men's concerns and experiences an integral dimension of the design, implementation, monitoring and evaluation of policies and programmes in all political, economic and societal spheres so that women and men benefit equally and inequality is not perpetuated.[19]

The way to mainstream gender in an effective manner is linking gender equality to the relevant sector. However, this cannot be undertaken in an ad hoc manner. The Office of the Special Advisor Report (2001) argues that for institutional development to be effective "developing guidelines, utilising gender specialists, providing competence development for all personnel, etc., is also required to support gender mainstreaming". A key factor that needs to be in place is buy-in from senior management. As described earlier, the UN Commission on the Status of Women advocates that responsibility for mainstreaming rests at the highest managerial levels. Therefore, without political will or support in organisations, mainstreaming would essentially be ineffective. Why then is the process of gender mainstreaming an important one? "Throughout the world, women suffer disadvantage. There are differences from country to country and region to region, because disadvantage is caused by cultural, historical and social factors."[20]

I have found that the most difficult barrier to overcome is that of political will. This factor is instrumental in achieving success. If senior management and essentially those with the power to influence resource allocation and create an enabling environment, do not have the political will to drive gender mainstreaming as a strategy for gender equality, the overall goal of any project or intervention will not be realised. I provide some broad guidelines and strategies that will assist you as a Human Resource practitioner and agent of agent, to overcome the major barrier of political will and to ultimately move your organisation towards an inclusive transformation strategy aimed at equal gender relations.

Gender mainstreaming is a strategy used to attain gender equality in the workplace and can be equated with transformation. Often transformation is only equated with issues of race and this is in fact incorrect. Diversity also, is often confused with race and this must also be addressed. As a Human Resource practitioner you must ask several questions that will inform your transformation strategy. Transformation means a profound change within an institution which, as a consequence, also affects the outside environment. It encompasses changes in the basic values and beliefs that are dominant in a certain institution, as well as changes in the rules and regulations that lead to certain working results. Processes of change within institutions occur continuously due to their changing environment, thus creating new demands or incentives for change. This change happens either unintentionally (thereby risking inefficiency), or in a planned and coordinated way, with executives acting as managers and coordinators.[21]

There are several phases of the transformation process. However, it is important to narrow these down to three key phases – the planning, implementation and consolidation phases. As explained earlier and reiterated throughout this book, the role and commitment of the executive staff across all management hierarchies is crucial for introducing and implementing gender mainstreaming. In this respect, their main responsibility is to adopt both the formal and informal mechanisms by which they usually create accountability and strengthen commitment, in order to ensure that all staff members are dedicated to gender mainstreaming.

Gender mainstreaming is led through a top-down approach with senior management being held accountable for the success or failure of gender mainstreaming as a strategy for gender equality. Senior management buy-in is not easy to attain and therefore must be lobbied by yourself as a Human Resource practitioner with the help of those who already believe in the message of gender equality and who currently have seats of power in your organisation. In the absence of such allies, you will have to make the case for gender equality on your own by considering the following:

★　Demonstrate how gender mainstreaming contributes to better achieving the organisation's mandate and goals (benefits of gender mainstreaming).

★　Have concrete suggestions on how to introduce and implement gender mainstreaming as a transformation strategy.

★　Understand possible concerns and constraints and consider how to address these in advance.

★　Find initial support from staff members in key positions (if none is forthcoming, revert to the other points provided here).

★　Approach managers who are thought most likely to support the initiative first.

You must consider the strengths and weaknesses of the current status quo at your organisation. Also think of the tangible and intangible barriers that exist to achieving gender quality. This will assist you in determining how to approach the planning phase. Undertake a SWOT analysis[22] before you commit to any sort of company action, whether you're exploring new initiatives, revamping internal policies, considering opportunities to pivot, or altering a plan midway through its execution.

> Performing a SWOT analysis is also a great way to improve business operations, said Andrew Schrage, partner and editor-in-chief of *Money Crashers*.[23]

Several factors in the SWOT analysis will inform how you approach your gender mainstreaming strategy for the achievement of gender equality in the workplace. Both internal and external factors are represented in the SWOT analysis.

The first two letters in the acronym, S (strengths) and W (weaknesses), refer to internal factors, which means the resources and experience readily available to you. Examples of areas typically considered include[24]:

★ Financial resources (funding, sources of income, investment opportunities).

★ Physical resources (location, facilities, equipment).

★ Human resources (employees, volunteers, target audiences).

★ Access to natural resources, trademarks, patents and copyrights.

★ Current processes (employee programmes, department hierarchies, software systems).

External factors influence and affect every company, organisation and individual. Whether these factors are connected directly or indirectly to an opportunity or threat, it is important to take note of and document each one. External factors typically reference things you or your organisation do not control, such as:

★ Market trends (new products and technology, shifts in audience needs).

★ Economic trends (local, national and international financial trends).

★ Funding (donations, legislature and other sources).

★ Demographics.

★ Relationships with suppliers and partners.

★ Political, environmental and economic regulations.

Example: JM Construction Law firm undertook a SWOT analysis aimed at implementing gender mainstreaming as a transformation strategy.

STRENGTHS

Construction law firm with staff members who are trained in both law and professional engineering/general contracting. Their experience gives a unique advantage.

Small (three employees) – can change and adapt quickly

WEAKNESSES

No one has been through any formal gender training programs.

One staff member has been a part of mediations but not as a neutral party in a sexual harassment case.

OPPORTUNITIES

Most commercial construction contracts require mediation. Despite hundreds of mediators in the marketplace only a few are aware of the importance of gender equality.

For smaller disputes, mediators don't work as a team, only as individuals; JM staff can offer anyone the advantage of a group of neutrals to evaluate a dispute.

THREATS

Anyone can become a mediator, so other construction law firms could open up their own mediation service as well and these could overtake the practice.

Most potential clients have a negative impression of mediation, because they feel mediators don't understand or care to understand the problem, and rush to resolve it without taking gender equality concerns into consideration.

> **Resulting strategy:** Take gender and diversity courses to eliminate weaknesses and launch JM Law Firm, highlighting that the firm understands the charged nature of the construction space for women.
>
> SWOT analysis forces the user to methodically and objectively look at what they had to work with and what the marketplace was offering.

Additional analytic tools to consider include PEST (political, economic, social and technological), MOST (mission, objective, strategies and tactics) and SCRS (strategy, current state, requirements and solution) analyses.

In approaching the implementation of gender mainstreaming you must consider the following key questions:

★ Is promoting gender equality part of the organisation's general focus?

★ Does the organisation have an official statement on their goal for gender equality and their strategy for pursuing gender mainstreaming? (this could also be part of your transformation strategy)

★ Is gender mainstreaming integrated in the regulations of the organisation and in both the formal and informal standard operating procedures?

★ Do the executive staff members demonstrate their commitment to gender equality and the implementation of gender mainstreaming, in both formal and informal ways?

★ Do the executive staff members exercise their responsibility for the implementation of gender mainstreaming, both by strengthening the commitment of all staff members and by adopting a gender equality perspective in their regular decision making?

In your planning phase you must realistically calculate the possible resources needed – both financial and human. It is the responsibility of an organisation's management to provide the necessary resources. Furthermore, allocating sufficient resources is a strong signal of the management's commitment to implementing gender mainstreaming. The workload of the gender mainstreaming support structure should be calculated. In organisations that already have gender equality staff, it is mostly they who are given the responsibility for introducing gender mainstreaming. This assignment of new tasks should be accompanied by a corresponding increase in the amount of working time made available for this purpose. Considerations need to be made regarding whether or not this can be achieved by redistributing other tasks, by extending working hours or by recruiting additional staff.

Some questions to consider when allocating both human and financial resources:

★ Does the expertise exist for the allocated team who will be responsible for the implementation of the gender mainstreaming strategy?

★ Have senior managers been allocated to the core team for the implementation of the gender equality projects?

★ Are the financial resources allocated for introducing gender mainstreaming realistically calculated and sufficient in order to ensure long-term success?

An organisational analysis is required through a gender audit. A gender audit is a participatory method for conducting an organisational analysis. It is a guided process of self-assessment supported by experienced facilitators, who raise key issues, enhance awareness about norms and attitudes and foster organisational learning. A gender audit is a sophisticated approach that addresses the cultural and informal aspects of an organisation's operation in particular. It aims at building ownership and promoting commitment to gender mainstreaming by involving as many staff as possible, for example, through a series of workshops and focus group meetings. This may be outsourced or undertaken by yourself. Consider the following elements when looking at your organisation[25]:

Table 2.1: Promoting internal commitment to Gender Mainstreaming

Gender mainstreaming support structure	Does the organisation already have a gender mainstreaming support structure?
	★ If so, is it capable of fulfilling all of its tasks successfully (e.g. with regard to its structure, resources, competences, position within the organisation)?
	★ If not, what structure is appropriate in terms of its tasks as well as the resources available?
	★ Which approach works best to successfully establish an effective support structure?
Gender equality objectives	★ Does the organisation have established and well-defined gender equality objectives?
	★ Which gender equality objectives are both ambitious and realistic for the organisation to pursue?
	★ What is the most effective and practicable way of developing and agreeing on gender equality objectives?
Communicating gender mainstreaming	★ Are all staff members aware of the intended process of organisational change?
	★ Are they well informed about both the planned activities, the reasons behind these and the aims of this process?
	★ What ways of communicating gender mainstreaming work best in order to ensure transparency and commitment?
	★ Is the organisation's public relations work gender sensitive in terms of language and illustrations?

Gender mainstreaming methods and tools	★ Have gender mainstreaming methods and tools already been developed and applied? What has worked well and what hasn't?
	★ In accordance with the organisation's regular practices, what are suitable methods for implementing gender mainstreaming?
	★ How and by whom should respective tools be developed?
	★ What are potential ways to introduce these?
Gender equality competence	★ Are all staff members committed to gender mainstreaming?
	★ Are they performing their respective tasks and following the rules of procedure in order to effectively implement gender mainstreaming?
	★ Do all staff members have the gender expertise and methodological skills they need to fulfil their responsibility for implementing gender mainstreaming?
	★ Which skills and knowledge need to be developed?
	★ What is the best approach to developing gender equality competence that will serve to strengthen commitment?
Gender information management system	★ Is information on gender issues available and easily accessible for staff members?
	★ What information is needed but missing?
	★ Are all statistics produced or used by the organisation gender disaggregated?
	★ What is an effective way of collecting and disseminating all information and data that is needed to ensure the well-substantiated implementation of gender mainstreaming?

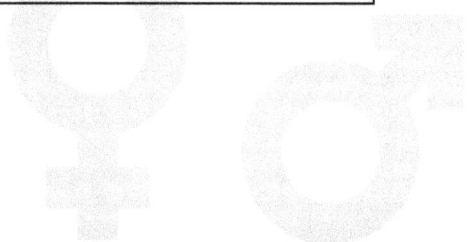

Gender equality action plans	★ Have all units of the organisation analysed gender issues in their particular fields of activity, operationalised gender equality objectives and developed approaches for addressing gender issues?
	★ What is an appropriate way to initiate and develop gender equality action plans in order to achieve this?
Equal opportunities within the organisation's personnel	★ What is the gender balance among staff throughout the organisation's different levels and fields of activity?
	★ Does the organisation have an equal opportunities plan to promote equal opportunities among its staff?
	★ What is an efficient strategy to promote equal opportunities within the organisation?
Monitoring and steering organisational change	★ Does the organisation have regular methods and procedures for monitoring and steering organisational processes?
	★ How will the process of organisational change towards gender mainstreaming be steered, and the progress monitored in an effective way?

What does the legislation reflect?[1]

As a Human Resource practitioner, it is important to understand the legislation influencing gender mainstreaming in South Africa. Institutionalising gender mainstreaming is emerging as the key to meaningful mainstreaming of gender. Gender mainstreaming highlights the inclusion of gender instead of women. Several key pieces of legislation must be considered by organisations across sectors. The Employment Equity Act of 1998 is an example of law reform seeking gender equality. Gender equality is explicitly stated in Section 2 as being achieved through the following:

---

1 Parts of this book have been submitted in the fulfilment of Doctor of Philosophy, Political Studies at the University of the Witwatersrand, December 2018.

Promoting equal opportunity and fair treatment in employment through the elimination of unfair discrimination; and

Implementing affirmative action measures to redress the disadvantages in employment experienced by designated groups, in order to ensure their equitable representation in all occupational categories and levels in the workforce.

The Employment Equity Act aimed to address gender equality in the employment of women and also sought to address injustices of the Apartheid system by allocating quota systems for race groups and people with disabilities.[26] In addition, the Promotion of Equality and Prevention of Unfair Discrimination Act of 2000 was passed into law and protects women, as reflected in Section 2. The Broad Based Black Economic Empowerment Act of 2004 also seeks to achieve the objective of gender equality under Section 2 and specific mention is made of ownership concerning women, participation of women in business etc. The Preferential Procurement Policy Framework Act of 2000 aims to implement reforms in the area of procurement. The Act addresses the area of gender equality in Section 2:(d)(i):

The specific goals may include: contracting with persons, or categories of persons, historically disadvantaged by unfair discrimination on the basis of race, gender or disability.

The Act specifies targets for women and people with disabilities. The Basic Conditions of Employment Act of 1997 is another piece of legislation attempting to address gender equality and advance social and economic justice. For the Public Service specifically, the National Policy Framework for Women Empowerment and Gender Equality was developed as the major policy ensuring that gender is mainstreamed within the State.

The creation of laws however does not necessarily translate into the elimination of gender discrimination. This is evidenced by the Beijing +20 Report 2014 which states that despite the South African State's progressive local legislative commitments to gender, women continue to be discriminated against. The Report,[27] goes further to explain:

Some of the laws also remain ambivalent or are inadequate to tackle systemic and structural discrimination and inequality such as in gender based violence, proprietary rights in marriage, particularly in respect of customary marriages concluded prior to 15 November 2000, hidden employment discrimination, land rights and access and economic inequalities. There is also some resistance to aspects of women's leadership, participation and representation.

Major obstacles as reported to the UN in the Beijing +20 Report show that there are several areas reflecting elements affecting gender equality including violence against women and girls. Ineffectiveness in mobilising around this social evil was attributed to poor access to resources (both human and financial). Gender-based violence against LGBTI communities was also viewed as a major obstacle in the South African State, answered by the establishment of a task team to address Hate Crime Legislation. The report also includes challenges around inadequate socio-economic empowerment for women.

Policies and programmatic measures have also been introduced. However, the poor implementation of these in some areas, or the lack of monitoring of these measures, or poor local governance have resulted in anomalies between different municipalities and delivery of basic services.[28]

Poverty specifically affecting women, and poor implementation of policy and organisational mechanisms have also been cited as major problems. Young African women attending the Beijing +10 Review claim that an "inclusive" approach was not adhered to. "However, we found that not only was the space of the Beijing +10 process not necessarily defined by the feminist and women's movements – the space was facilitated by the UN".[29] The latter speaks to the dichotomy of being player and referee in the global gender equality struggle.

In the National Gender Survey conducted by the Commission for Gender Equality in South Africa, Julien and Majake[30] believe that the findings reflect a reaffirmation that a gap exists between policy and implementation. They recommend that, "... more vigorous intervention is needed for repositioning feminist knowledge and development." This is supported by Moletsane[31] in her assessment of South Africa's progress towards equality in Education and Grant[32] in her analysis of women in the South African workplace. Van der Westhuizen[33] adds to the gender equality debate, by affirming that "... at the bottom of gender inequality lies power – who has it, but most decisively, how it is exercised."

28

The Beijing +20 report is also supported by the *Towards a Fifteen Year Review* (2009), arguing that:

> While these institutional arrangements for driving the issues of gender equality tend to be acknowledged internationally as best practice, closer to home one finds challenges in their operation. Chief among these is the matter of entrenched negative attitudes towards gender equality, lack of understanding and accountability to address this coherently, and inadequate mechanisms and resourcing, financially and in terms of human capacity, for effective implementation. Related to this is a problem of policy frameworks without legal status that are therefore not legally binding.

Comparatively, Chukwuemeka,[34] in her discussion on the Nigerian case, states that policy implementation has become the focus, after realising that effective implementation is not an automatic. This is comparative to the case of South Africa, given the major challenges experienced in implementing key legislative commitments discussed thus far. Roux,[35] in her analysis of policy formulation and implementation, looks at how South Africa is held accountable to a set of standards set by international agreements: "...Government is obliged to constantly measure its national policies and programmes against international, or global, best practices and requirements."

Ultimately, policies formulated by the South African State and the main international legislative commitments, are aimed at change. However, several elements need to be in place to effect this. To this end, Roux[36] claims: "Real transformation can only successfully occur when the majority of individuals in political and executive organisations change their mindsets, behaviour and corporate culture. Everything is involved, from structures and systems, management styles, core competencies and worker profiles, to core outputs required."

It is important to provide a balanced view of using gender mainstreaming as a strategy for gender equality in the workplace. Human Resource practitioners must be made aware of the shortcomings to ensure they are prepared to circumvent and/or manage expectations. Johnsson-Latham[37] lists elements that have generally been noted as problems. Most relevant to the gender mainstreaming is the conclusion that due to the absence of commitment, funding and human resources, gender mainstreaming has been reduced to a technique rather than an important integral process. Most notably, the patriarchal attitudes of both men and women in the workplace pose the biggest threat to gender mainstreaming as a strategy for gender equality.

Alston[38] claims that some evidence suggests that gender mainstreaming is poorly understood by many in higher positions of power. As a result, women, particularly at grassroots level, do not always benefit from gender mainstreaming. Hannan[39] states that since 1995, a number of serious misconceptions around gender mainstreaming have developed, hampering the effective implementation of the strategy. These are sometimes linked to the lack of knowledge of concepts such as "gender" and "gender equality". Rather the major discussion is focused on the role of political will in ensuring that there is a common understanding and approach at an organisation to the implementation of gender mainstreaming initiatives and, by implication, a common understanding of gender and gender equality.

Leyenaar[40] raises an issue that relates to the attitude adopted towards engendering policies. She highlights that the political will to achieve greater equality by incorporating a gender perspective in policies is not a matter of routine. Wendoh and Wallace[41] in their analysis of African countries' attention to gender mainstreaming, note that officials at higher management echelons give priority to their own activities and consider gender issues to have less value. Lyons[42] argues that gender as a specific cultural construct, varies from culture to culture. These arguments resonate with the book and inform how officials at higher management echelons have a major influence on the outcomes of initiatives in organisations.

In effect, this means that those whose responsibility it is to mainstream gender must be cautious of using a one-size-fits-all approach, as every situation has its unique opportunities and challenges. A similar study undertaken by the Department of Water Affairs in implementing gender mainstreaming into operations (2006–2010) revealed that there is a marginalisation of gender.

Gender mainstreaming is viewed as a non-core function. As a result, officials working on gender mainstreaming struggle to make sure that issues related to gender mainstreaming are taken seriously. Moser[43] posits that the ultimate test of whether gender mainstreaming has either succeeded or failed lies in the rigorous monitoring and evaluation tools. For Moser, the biggest challenge lies in identifying correct indicators, which would require four interrelated indicators measuring inputs, outputs, effects and impacts.

A 2004 IDASA paper[44] also highlights that for States, National Gender Machineries face financial challenges as they are often under-resourced and unable to operate on the inadequate budget allocated to them. As Clisby[45] points out, much still needs to be addressed to ensure that gender mainstreaming is translated into tangible results on the ground. She cautions that unless this is done, gender mainstreaming becomes semantics co-opted by politicians and policy-makers. Riley[46] also states that experience in organisations has indicated that changing from gender mainstreaming as a policy to implementing or practising gender mainstreaming has been challenging. Riley notes amongst others, the need for practical training on gender mainstreaming.

Gender Desks

In the public sector, dedicated gender desks are often established within a Department. These desks are usually run by what is named in the South African Public Service a "Gender Focal Point". This person is responsible for the mainstreaming of gender in the relevant Department. The establishment of the Department of Women has somewhat blurred this role and many Gender Focal Points are now managing portfolios that include gender, HIV/AIDS, Disability and Diversity. Some Departments also include the function of gender mainstreaming under Employee Health and Wellness, meaning that many of the intended dedicated desks have several competing priorities and importantly, limited resources.

In my experience of rolling out gender mainstreaming initiatives within the South African State I have found that Gender Focal Points are under-resourced in terms of financial and human resources. The competing priorities have had a major influence on the ability of Gender Focal Points to reach their goals. Coupled with the lack of resources was the lack of political will by those with the power to unblock barriers and support gender mainstreaming initiatives. This experience reiterates the need for senior management support as described earlier in this chapter.

Gender Focal Points also face the barrier of bureaucracy as many are situated at middle management level. It is imperative for those responsible for the rollout of gender mainstreaming as a strategy for gender equality, to ensure that the person/s are situated at a senior management level to influence the availing of resources (both human and financial) to create an enabling environment for the overall goal of gender equality in the workplace.

Gender Desks may be a suitable option for Human Resource practitioners. However, the onus is on the organisation to appoint a person at a high level and ensure that this person has access to the necessary forums, such as the Executive Committee meetings, to push the gender agenda. It is my opinion that a dedicated Gender Desk with adequate resourcing can ensure that gender mainstreaming strategies are in fact successful in achieving gender equality in the workplace. The necessary political will must be present both at an operational level and at a strategic level in order for Gender Desks to be successful.

Post et al.[47] claims that "political will" is an ambiguous term. They go further to claim that the manner in which the term "political will" is used is a reflection of how it is used in achieving policy change. "Plainly speaking, political will is the extent of committed support among key decision-makers for a particular policy solution to a particular problem."

Post et al.[48] argue that the factors affecting the presence and/or absence of political will is directly dependent on whether adequate decision-makers exist and whether these decision-makers have an informed understanding of a particular problem and have adopted a formal agenda. Notably, they also argue that these decision-makers must be committed to supporting the agenda and there must be an effective policy solution. The commitment of decision-makers is the overriding factor in the success of gender projects. It is therefore important that Human Resource practitioners are part of the decision-making process in order to ensure the success of gender projects in an organisation.

Kapoutsis et al.,[49] in their multi-study of political will, found that political will is the primary motivator for mobilising personal and organisational resources to achieve political goals. They further identify that there are two major political motivators, namely the self-serving and the benevolent. The role of the self-serving and benevolent actions by an individual cannot be assessed in this book. However, the presence of these factors must be noted as influencing elements in the decisions of those who have power in an organisation.

Political will is expressed as political behaviour but behaviour is influenced by various factors. Many studies confirm that in the life of an individual, values and value systems represent the main influences in political behaviour.[50] Values possess the most influence on views and behaviours.[51] These are used as the criteria for evaluating people and events. Values are central in politics and political judgements as well as preferences.[52] The values of an individual in an organisation and the values of the organisation have a direct influence on the success of projects aimed at transformation.

Schwartz[53] defines political will as "ideas or beliefs related to desirable goals or behaviours that go beyond specific situations, guide selection or evaluation of behaviour and events and which are hierarchically ordered by relative importance to an individual." The behaviour of individuals ultimately influences the outcome of the gender projects at the Department. This is evident from my own observations in the field and is a reflection of the need to promote values-based leadership as discussed in later chapters.

Senior management therefore is a critical component to the creation of an enabling environment and must be approached formally through their performance agreements, the development and approval of a Gender Action Plan and finally the establishment of a high-level dedicated Gender Desk. Senior management efforts cannot however be viewed on their own; political will, as discussed above, must also emanate from operational staff in the implementation of gender mainstreaming as a strategy for gender equality.

Gender Action Plan

A gender action plan is a tangible tool used to ensure that gender is mainstreamed within organisations. This includes clear targets, quotas, gender design features and quantifiable performance indicators to ensure women's participation and benefits. Priority areas for the development of a Gender Action Plan will be based on the needs of your organisation.

Case study on LEGO

CASE STUDY

CEO of LEGO, Jørgen Vig Knudstorp, describes how the LEGO organization's initial internal changes were caused by grass root initiatives led by female employees, who e.g. organized networking groups and events for the women in the organization (Ligestilling and DI). This illustrates the trend that highly educated Danish women are now, more than before, organizing in communities across industries and are in that way helping each other to get ahead.[54]

It is your duty as the Human Resource Practitioner to provide means for the proverbial levelling of the playing field. Based on the 2018 McKinsey study on Women in the Workplace, women face everyday discrimination. Women experience micro-aggressions in the workplace in the form of sexism and racism. This takes many forms. Some can be subtle, like when a person mistakenly assumes a co-worker is more junior than they really are. Some are more explicit, like when a person says something demeaning to a co-worker. Whether intentional or unintentional, micro-aggressions signal disrespect.

Most commonly, women have to provide more evidence of their competence than men and they have their judgement questioned in their area of expertise. They are also twice as likely as men to have been mistaken for someone in a more junior position. Black women, in particular, deal with a greater variety of micro-aggressions and are more likely than other women to have their judgement questioned in their area of expertise and be asked to provide additional evidence of their competence.

Seventy-one percent have dealt with micro-aggressions. The nature of these encounters is often different for them: lesbian women are far more likely than other women to hear demeaning remarks in the workplace about themselves or others like them. They are also far more likely to feel like they cannot talk about their personal lives at work.

A third of lesbian women feel like they can't talk about themselves or their life outside of work.[55]

Micro-aggressions aren't only for women. About half of men have experienced micro-aggressions, and the problem is worse for men of colour and gay men. Black men, like Black women, are more likely to have their judgement questioned and be asked to provide more evidence of their qualifications. Gay men, like lesbian women, are far more likely to hear demeaning remarks about themselves or others like them and to feel discouraged from talking about their personal lives at work.[56] In the McKinsey study of Women in the Workplace, the following was revealed in an assessment of 64000 employees and has been adapted for the South African context:

Table 2.2: Current Status of Women in the Workplace

Question	All Men	All Women	White Women	Asian Women	Black Women	Lesbian Women
Having your judgement questioned in your area of expertise	27%	36%	36%	29%	40%	37%
Needing to provide more evidence of your competence than others do	16%	31%	29%	36%	42%	34%
Being addressed in a less-than-professional way	16%	26%	26%	21%	26%	23%
Being mistaken for someone at a much lower level	10%	20%	19%	22%	22%	20%
Often having your work contributions ignored	16%	17%	16%	16%	22%	20%
Hearing demeaning remarks about you or people like you	10%	16%	16%	15%	19%	26%

The study conducted above did not look at the cross-pollination of issues such as race and the marginalisation of lesbian women. These statistics are still alarming and must be addressed.

> "I walked into a meeting where I was the only woman in a very large room of men. And when I sat down, an older white man from another company turned to me out of nowhere and said, 'Could you take notes for the meeting?' Which was a little bit odd because I was the lawyer in the room, the one doing the negotiating." —VP, 6 years at company, Middle Eastern woman.[57]

Consider the following checklist for a Diversity strategy that includes race, disability and gender equality.[58]

Table 2.3: Checklist for developing a Diversity strategy

Theme	Target	Progress
Gender		
Race		
Disability		
Gender & Race Combined		
Development of Matrices for the Measurement of Diversity		
Reports by Senior Management on Compliance with Targets		

Reflect on the case study below for a possible approach to influencing how senior managers approach the representation of women.

Case study: VMware: Tracking and Rewarding Progress

What they did:

VMware wanted to make diversity metrics easy for senior leaders to access and to hold them accountable for improving the metrics. VMware's CEO gave each vice president a yearly goal of improving the global representation of women. To develop strategic action plans, VPs were given access to a diversity dashboard with real-time HR metrics. The dashboard tracks representation, hiring, promotions, and retention, showing areas of progress in green and areas of decline in red. This tool helped leaders to easily see improvement areas, strategise, and track progress toward meeting their representation targets. Each senior leader's progress is recorded on a scorecard and reviewed at regular intervals with the CEO's executive staff. To meet their business goals, senior leaders now have to meet representation targets and demonstrate inclusive behaviour.

Outcomes:

Since announcing these goals and unveiling the dashboard in August 2017, VMware has made significant progress. Their global hiring rate for women is 5.6 percentage points higher than their baseline representation, and for the past twelve months, the company has met gender representation targets across all geographic regions.

The African Development Bank has produced several guidelines that are useful for inclusion in your considerations for the development of a Gender Action Plan to assist you with your mainstreaming initiatives. They claim that the Gender Action Plan is a key mainstreaming tool. It gives visibility to and accountability for gender mainstreaming. They make gender mainstreaming tangible and explicit in programme and project design and implementation. These plans include quotas and targets. There are several myths around the operationalisation of a Gender Action Plan; some centre on the theory that these are separate plans. Nothing could be further from the truth. When undertaking transformation, one has to look at how the strategies for such transformation can be embedded into everyday tasks and major projects in order to implement sustainable change. Gender Action Plans must be closely aligned with project outputs. They are an integral part of the project design, financing and implementation. Monitoring and Evaluation must also be specifically mainstreamed for gender equality. This is discussed in Chapter 7.

An example of a Gender Action Plan follows adapted from the United Nations Fund for Climate Change:[59]

Table 2.4: An example of a Gender Action Plan

Priority Area: Gender balance			
Activities	**Responsible Actors**	**Timeline**	**Deliverables**
Provide capacity-building to Chairs and senior management on how to integrate gender considerations into their respective areas of work and on meeting the goal of gender balance	Office of the CEO Human Resources Senior Management	June 2019	Provision of capacity-building Chairs and senior management supporting the integration of gender into their work
Through the use of such mechanisms as workshops, technical assistance, etc., enhance the capacity of staff to develop gender-responsive policies, plans and programmes	Human Resources Senior and Middle Management	November 2019	Gender-responsive policies, plans and programmes
Mainstreaming of gendered indicators and targets into staff performance agreements	Human Resources Office of the CEO	May 2019	Gender-responsive performance agreements

High-quality Gender Action Plans result in:

★ Increased participation of women in activities

★ More equitable access to project and programme resources

★ Increased income for women which is the most practical benefit

The Gender Action Plan provides a step-by-step process for you as a Human Resource practitioner to follow. These plans can be adapted and replicated in different sectors, thus increasing the scope of transformation.

Several best practices have emerged for the private sector in South Africa developed by the 30% Club in collaboration with the Department of Women, titled "Best Practices in Gender Mainstreaming".[60] They suggest that gender mainstreaming must be compatible with the other strategies of the organisation, meaning that this cannot be a stand-alone strategy that does not have links to the existing way of working. Importantly, the 30% Club suggests that the strategies must be fitting for the particular type of organisation and the environment that the organisation is working in. Best Practice number 16 is noteworthy:

> Where an organisation is required to have a Social & Ethics Committee in terms of the Companies Act 2008, such committee should ensure that all of its members are well versed in Gender Mainstreaming both in terms of legislation, regulations and the international business case.[61]

Best Practice number 16 essentially advocates for mainstreaming at levels of the organisation. The Report goes further to recommend that private sector organisations consider the suitability of women from outside the corporate mainstream for non-executive positions. It suggests that these could include professionals, successful entrepreneurs, non-profit executives, and academics. In terms of management practices, it is suggested that management is encouraged to build up a track record of sourcing, developing and advancing women within the organisation

Flexible working programmes are also addressed in the Best Practices with specific reference to number 45: "Address the stigma that flexibility signals low career ambition and commitment. Organisations should make women aware of the negative connotations with working within an established flexibility programme." This practice is of particular relevance for a more sensitised working environment as the flexibility associated with working hours is often begrudged by employees who do not have family responsibilities. 'Family' here is defined loosely and entails responsibility for those who are within their household and may not necessarily only constitute their children but rather all their dependants. Finally, and perhaps the most important inclusion as resonates with the report discussed earlier by the South African Human Rights Commission, the issue of gender pay gaps must be addressed. These Best Practices emanate from the South African context, and you are encouraged to review these practices and unearth what you feel could be of use to your organisation.

As part of your Gender Action Plan, you need to consider how you will embed your actions into the organisational systems and thus mainstream gender for gender equality.

Table 2.5: Assessing organisational systems for gender mainstreaming interventions

Area of Intervention[62]	Activities
Integrate gender equity into existing strategic plans, policies, and practices	Integrating gender equity into existing strategic plans, policies and practices creates a workplace environment, culture and conditions that support gender equity. ★ Focus on integrating gender equity in strategic documents that hold considerable influence on organisational priorities and actions and that place a sense of accountability on the workplace through internal and external reporting. ★ Aim to integrate gender equity into organisational frameworks, to help ensure that other policies and plans under that framework also consider gender equity. ★ Align gender equity with the purpose and key priorities of existing strategies and policies. ★ Include multi-year commitments within strategies to address gender equity and prevent violence against women, to ensure activities to deliver on these commitments occur over multiple years.

Area of Intervention[62]	Activities
Integrate gender equity into existing strategic plans, policies, and practices (cont.)	★ Be aware of key processes and timeframes that impact the development and updating of workplace policies and strategic documents. Develop relationships with staff responsible for these strategies. ★ Be mindful that consultations to develop strategies are key processes to build awareness and capacity to promote gender equity. ★ Seek expert advice from organisations or individuals as needed.
Develop a gender equity or preventing violence against women strategy	Developing a stand-alone strategy on gender equity or the prevention of violence against women may help workplaces to achieve an integrated, whole-of-organisation approach to gender equity. Developing, implementing and monitoring strategies requires commitment and skilled staff.
Embed gender equity within Human Resources	Working with Human Resources might help ensure that efforts to change organisational cultures to better support gender equity and respect are also reflected in human resources policies and processes. Possible actions that could be implemented by Human Resources include the following: ★ Inclusion of a family violence leave and support clause in the organisation's enterprise agreement. These clauses aim to support staff experiencing family violence and provide a consistent and positive approach to responding to disclosures of family violence. ★ Training of Human Resources staff to understand the impacts of family violence in the workplace, the gendered nature of family violence and the supports available to staff experiencing family violence. ★ Applying a gender lens to human resources policies that are being reviewed or developed, to ensure the policy supports gender equity. For example, ensuring that part-time workers have access to study support and opportunities for higher duties, consideration of how unconscious bias might affect recruitment, and promoting flexible work policies to women and men. See: Applying a gender lens in the workplace at vichealth.vic.gov.au/GEAR-tools for more information.

Area of Intervention[62]	Activities
Embed gender equity within Human Resources (cont.)	★ Providing leadership and administrative support for training and events on preventing violence against women and gender equity.
Establish supportive workplace structures	Supportive workplace structures such as networks, committees and working groups can help to embed gender equity in organisations. These groups may have a sole focus on gender equity and preventing violence against women, or consider gender equity as one component of a broader remit. Committees can play an important role in the following: ★ Driving and sustaining activity to create gender equity. ★ Acting as a consultation mechanism for gender equity activity. ★ Ensuring that organisations are accountable and act on their stated commitments. ★ Engaging workplace champions. Consider expanding the remit of an existing committee to include gender equity, or establishing a new committee. It is important to ensure a diverse range of stakeholders are represented in its membership. A gender balance for membership is encouraged.

Senior management is a critical component to the creation of an enabling environment and must be approached formally through their performance agreements, the development and approval of a Gender Action Plan and finally the establishment of a high-level dedicated Gender Desk. Senior management efforts cannot however be viewed on their own. Political will, as discussed above, must also emanate from operational staff in the implementation of gender mainstreaming as a strategy for gender equality. In order to ensure that political will is gained, consider the case study below focused on local government transformation for gender equality.

Case Study [63]

The City of Monash is a local government area in Melbourne, Victoria, Australia in the south-eastern suburbs of Melbourne with an area of 81.0 square kilometres and a population of 182,618 people in 2016. This case was selected as it reflects the embodiment of gender equity into local government plans and is an efficient example of how gender equality can be operationalised.

Embedding gender equity into the strategic plans of local government

The table below shows how Monash City Council embedded gender equity into a number of their strategic plans of local government.

Gender equity was integrated into a number of existing strategic plans, policies and practices and a new strategy was created to support Council to achieve an integrated, whole-of-organisation approach to gender equity.

Strategy	Strategic document	Reference to gender equity and preventing violence against women
Integrate gender equity into existing strategic plans, policies, and practices	Council Plan 2013–2017 www.monash. vic.gov.au/About-Us/ Council/Publications/ Council-Plan	A key community outcome is 'Communities and organisations promote respect and equality and prevent violence against women'. The strategy to achieve this outcome was to 'implement the Generating Equality and Respect program, which aims to build equal and respectful relationships between men and women and prevent violence against women'.
	Access and Equity Framework 2013–2017 www.monash. vic.gov.au/About-Us/ Council/Publications/ Access-and-Equity	Gender equity was integrated into Council's Access and Equity Framework. As this framework includes a number of Council policies relating to social justice, integration into this framework helped to ensure that other Council policies and plans under this framework were also considered gender equity.

Strategy	Strategic document	Reference to gender equity and preventing violence against women
		The framework articulates that "Council has a role to play in the development of a socially just, healthy, inclusive and sustainable community where all members irrespective of their ability, gender, social, ethnic, or economic background can fully and fairly participate in community life. This framework will ensure that all Council policies and strategies consider and integrate these rights-based principles." **CASE STUDY** Embedding gender equity into the strategic plans of local government The table below shows how Monash City Council embedded gender equity into a number of their strategic plans of local government. Gender equity was integrated into a number of existing strategic plans, policies and practices and a new strategy was created to support Council in achieving an integrated, whole-of-organisation approach to gender equity.
	Monash Youth Plan 2013–2016 www.monash.vic.gov.au/About-Us/Council/Publications/Plans-and-Strategies/Youth-Plan	Two actions in the Youth Plan recognise the role of local government in preventing violence against women, specifically with young people. These include 'Develop a Positive Peer Relationship initiative for young people in Years 7 and 8 using a whole-school approach', and 'Enhance youth service providers' capacity to deliver good practice, respectful relationships, and education'.

Strategy	Strategic document	Reference to gender equity and preventing violence against women
Develop a gender equity or preventing violence against women strategy	Gender Equity Strategy 2015–2020 http://www.monash.vic.gov.au/About-Us/ Council/Publications/ Plans-and-Strategies/ Gender-Equity-Strategy	The Gender Equity Strategy aims to support Council to achieve an integrated, whole-of-organisation approach to gender equity. It will ensure that gender equity is considered and prioritised in all current and future Council planning, policy, service delivery and practice. The vision of the Strategy is for an inclusive and gender-equitable city, where females and males are treated with respect and have equal opportunities, decision-making power and responsibilities, regardless of their gender. The Strategy sits under the Access and Equity Framework, which ensures the Gender Equity Strategy considers other elements of diversity and equity, and that other Council strategies also consider gender equity.

Building an organisational culture that supports gender equity is critical to creating a gender-equitable workplace. A supportive organisational culture helps to create and sustain an 'authorising environment' for change. A workplace culture that supports gender equity can be seen in organisations that are:

★ Aware of the importance of gender equality and respectful relationships and their current performance.

★ Ready to talk about gender inequality, gender stereotypes, and violence against women.

★ Open to doing things differently.

★ Committed to taking action to build a fairer workplace.

This chapter highlights the importance of building a supportive community for gender equality both internal and external to the organisation. It is important to consider using men as agents of change and to follow an inclusive process so that employees are informed in a transparent manner.

The next chapter looks at what works in the mainstreaming of gender as a strategy for gender equality, looking at other state and private sector experiences.

CHAPTER 3

What Works? Reflecting on Cases for Gender Mainstreaming

Whilst South Africa has major legislation governing the implementation of gender mainstreaming, it is important to reflect on what other countries have achieved and how this can be applied to our context. South Africa has retrogressed in crucial global indices but narrowly made the top 20 countries in the World Economic Forum's (WEF) Global Gender Gap Report for 2017. The Global Gender Index ranks countries according to calculated gender gap between women and men in four key areas – health, education, economy and politics – to gauge the state of gender equality in a country. The report measures women's disadvantage compared to men, and is not strictly a measure of equality. Gender imbalances to the advantage of women do not affect the score [2]. So, for example, the indicator "number of years of a female head of state (last 50 years) over male value" would score 1 if the number of years was 25, but would still score 1 if the number of years was 50. Due to this methodology, gender gaps that favour women over men are reported as equality and would not cause deficits of equality in other areas to become less visible in the score, except for life expectancy.[64]

The three highest-ranking countries have closed over 84% of their gender gaps, while the lowest-ranking country has closed only a little over 50% of its gender gap. It "assesses countries on how well they are dividing their resources and opportunities among their male and female populations, regardless of the overall levels of these resources and opportunities," the

Report says. "By providing a comprehensible framework for assessing and comparing global gender gaps and by revealing those countries that are role models in dividing these resources equitably between women and men, the Report serves as a catalyst for greater awareness as well as greater exchange between policymakers."

The report examines four overall areas of inequality between men and women in 130 economies around the globe, over 93% of the world's population:

★ Economic participation and opportunity – outcomes on salaries, participation levels and access to high-skilled employment.

★ Educational attainment – outcomes on access to basic and higher-level education.

★ Political empowerment – outcomes on representation in decision-making structures.

★ Health and survival – outcomes on life expectancy and sex ratio. In this case parity is not assumed, there are assumed to be fewer female births than male (944 female for every 1,000 males), and men are assumed to die younger. Provided that women live at least 6% longer than men, parity is assumed. But if it is less than 6% it counts as a gender gap.

Thirteen out of the fourteen variables used to create the index are from publicly available "hard data" indicators from international organisations, such as the International Labour Organization, the United Nations Development Programme and the World Health Organization. The highest possible score is 1.0 (equality or better for women, except for lifespan [106% or better for women] and gender parity at birth [94.4% or better for women]) and the lowest possible score is 0. Data for some countries are unavailable.

Table 3.1: South Africa's year-on-year Gender Equality Score

Country	2014	2015	2016	2017	2018
South Africa	0.7527	0.759	0.764	0.756	0.755

Note: The highest possible score on the index is 1.

The country fell four places to 19 of 144 countries covered in the flagship report this year. The continent's most advanced economy ranked the third most gender-equal country in sub-Saharan Africa behind Rwanda and Namibia, which featured at numbers 4 and 16 respectively. In the bottom three spots of the global index were war-torn Syria, ranked 142, Pakistan at 143 and Yemen, one of the Arab world's poorest countries, rock bottom at 144. On sub-Saharan Africa, the index noted that the region, with an average remaining gender gap of 32%, "scores in the lower middle range of the Global Gender Gap Index".[65]

According to the index 56.1% of all South African women's work was unpaid, compared to 25.9% of men. This staggering figure is noteworthy when approaching a gender equality strategy for your organisation. The huge unpaid labour burden on women must be noted as an additional factor when assessing how to approach a gender mainstreaming strategy. Although South Africa seems to rank well, the 2017 report reflects a decline and a widening of the gender gap since its inception in 2006. Behind the decline is a widening of the gender gap across all four of the report's pillars: Educational Attainment, Health and Survival, Economic Opportunity and Political Empowerment. These latter two areas are of particular concern because they already carry the largest gaps and, until this year, were registering the fastest progress.

Country case studies

Rathgeber[66] argues "...some agencies have regarded gender mainstreaming as a goal that can be achieved through the provision of appropriate training materials, guidelines and checklists for their staff. However, experience has shown that gender mainstreaming cannot be achieved without active involvement by senior managers." Rathgeber's experience is echoed in my own experience of implementing the gender mainstreaming initiatives within the South African State. This has by and large been a difficult task as the buy-in of senior management is key to the initiatives of any organisation trying to mainstream gender. The lesson that emerged is that regardless of resource allocation for training and capacity-building interventions, training is but one piece of a larger proverbial pie.

Globally, other governments have noted that organisational mechanisms must be developed in order for gender to be effectively mainstreamed. This shift is largely due to pressure from the United Nations (UN). Rai[67] states that:

> States' acceptance of the outcome of the world conferences on women, particularly the BPFA and the outcome document of the twenty-third special session of the Gender Assembly on Gender Equality, Development and Peace for the Twenty-First Century, has resulted in commitment to some form of institutional change.

Madrid[68] adds to the debate by arguing that though much attention has been paid to gender equity, this issue has not been adequately addressed by countries seeming to be in compliance with the requirements of international treaties. Madrid therefore supports the notion that countries are complying with legalistic requirements for gender mainstreaming in a very limited manner, thus rendering gender mainstreaming efforts ineffectual. Compliance is highlighted in this book as a major element in limiting gender mainstreaming initiatives.

Gender equity has become a public issue since the UN Decade for Women (1975–1985). Several countries have provided different emphasis to this problem. Other countries have developed broad gender policies and mechanisms while still others have partial and sometimes incoherent actions.[69]

Madrid[70] notes that the implementation of policies advocated by the Women's National Service (SERNAM) does not interface with the policies of the Chilean Department of Education, rendering Chile's educational policies insensitive to gender. Without this close synergy, other role-players, such as the Chilean Catholic Church, regulate a more conservative policy, especially in the area of sexual health.[71] That said, Chile has had notable success in the mainstreaming of gender in other areas. The establishment of the Council of Ministers on Equal Opportunity and the inclusion of gender as a focus in the Ministry for Finance signify progress, particularly in the former where "equal opportunity" is informed by the Equal Opportunity Plan for Women and Men (Report on Implementation of the Beijing Platform for Action presented by the Government of Chile to the UN Division for the Advancement of Women[72]).

Programmes in Uganda were affected by factors such as insensitivity, poorly rendered gender disaggregated data and limited financial resources, amongst others. These factors result in poor gender responsiveness and poor gender-sensitive development practice.[73] Similar cultural problems are faced in South Africa.[74] Once again, the need for organisational mechanisms for the effective mainstreaming of gender is emphasised, because social and cultural stereotypes still treat gender mainstreaming as a women's issue. There is a glaring failure to implement seemingly progressive legislation.

Mexico faces similar barriers to the mainstreaming of gender in its energy sector, particularly in the Department of Technical Co-operation. Like Uganda, this male-dominated sector struggles to mainstream gender due to a lack of organisational mechanisms. Rathgeber[75] explains that in the Department of Technical Co-operation there are glaring problems with the recruitment of female scientists:

> Often women and girls are steered away from careers in science. It is therefore necessary to build a base of female scientists to counterbalance this.[76]

Rathgeber[77] claims that women are deliberately excluded from the recruitment process, based on ideas as to what "qualified" means. She advocates the need for a clear understanding of what "qualified" is defined as and maintains that the area of management experience needs to be revised in order to provide equal opportunities. In the case of Mexico, women were delayed in achieving their management experience in the field of nuclear energy and this must not be recognised as a shortcoming for such candidates in the recruitment process.

Rathgeber[78] advocates that the Department of Technical Co-operation must work closely with the national women's machinery and provide support for gender mainstreaming to be effective. The author claims that national machineries must be given necessary support in terms of resourcing and skills in order for gender equality to be achieved.

Furthermore, she recommends the need for a gender action plan that is institutionalised at all levels of the Department of Technical Co-operation in order for the mainstreaming of gender to be effective. The development of a gender action plan and the implementation thereof is a key piece of the gender equality journey. The Gender Action Plan must be prioritised by your organisation as the necessary tool for transformation as this effectively makes mainstreaming everyone's responsibility. Mexico's recommendations resonate with those proposed by both Chile and Uganda. Seemingly, although there is a commitment to gender mainstreaming on paper, these paper rights are not being translated into reality. Patriarchy still dominates the daily operations of government departments.[79] These findings are similar to the experiences in all sectors as noted in the Global Gender Gap Report discussed earlier. The experiences of those in the State are echoed in other sectors.

In the case of the Caribbean, a study was done on 10 countries namely: Montserrat, St. Kitts and Nevis, Saint Lucia, Barbados, Belize, Guyana, Jamaica, Saint Vincent and the Grenadines, Suriname and Trinidad and Tobago by Harris, Kambon and Clarke in 2000, funded by the Canadian International Development Agency. None of the machineries were originally given the primary mandate as an advocacy unit to influence the planning processes across development sectors. This meant that the machineries were removed from actual planning and operations. Despite the rhetoric of gender mainstreaming, the machineries remain distant from the ministries of planning.[80] We can learn from these experiences by noting that gender mainstreaming committees must be constituted and have influence over operations.

Many of these barriers noted in this chapter are shared by the South African State. The obstacles cited in the case above included:

★   Uncertainty about the role of the bureau.

★   Poor access to human and financial resources.

★   Poor administrative capability within the public service bureaucracy.

★   Lack of co-operation of administrators in instrumental sectors of the economy.

★   Poor monitoring mechanisms.

52

The barriers as indicated by Harris, Kambon and Clarke[81] resonate with the experience of gender desks in the South African State. Notably, other countries face similar obstacles in the mainstreaming of gender.

Mehra and Gupta[82] argue, however, that it is too soon to assess the effectiveness of gender projects, since much of the mainstreaming has not been sufficiently supported to be realised. Many elements such as human resources and engendered indicators are precursors to success.

At the Fourth World Conference for Women in 1995, gender mainstreaming was adopted as a major strategy for gender equality; however, this is not an end in itself. Mainstreaming of gender at an operational level needs to take into account key drivers both within and outside government. This, in effect, means that governments need to mainstream gender into their work and a paradigm shift is needed to achieve this. From the cases discussed, it is noted that gender mainstreaming is mostly adequately addressed at policy level and that glaring failings are evident at implementation level. This can be seen especially in previously male-dominated arenas where patriarchal ideology prevails.

The case of Jamaica is also comparative to the South African experience of mainstreaming when one assesses how the implementation of gender mainstreaming was approached. The National Policy for Gender Equality[83] stipulates the elements and pieces needed to enable the successful mainstreaming of gender into their society.

> The Government of Jaimaica (GOJ) shall establish Gender Focal Points (GFPs) in all ministries, departments and agencies (MDAs). Gender Focal Points shall act as responsibility centres in order to improve organizational effectiveness and capacity within the public sector. They shall develop, implement and monitor gender-sensitive policies, plans, programming and projects within their respective MDAs and contribute to the coordination of critical information needed to fulfil local, regional and international requirements. GFPs shall be of high enough rank to be able to be effective in their roles and for them to have consistent influence on their organizations. Each GFP shall be responsible for reporting their progress to the Permanent Secretary or Executive Officer of his/her MDA while also reporting on a quarterly basis to the Executive Director of the Bureau for Women's Affairs (BWA).

This experience is very similar to structures produced by the South African State in terms of the appointment of GFPs and the establishment of the BWA. However, what can be learnt from the Jamaican experience is the distinct difference in implementation. There is a clear need to regulate reporting at a political level and ensure that reporting does not remain at compliance level by ensuring that information is fed directly into the BWA which is the equivalent of the Department of Women in South Africa. This distinction ensures that accurate statistical information and qualitative research can be informed for each sector in the fulfilment of local, regional and international commitments. The South African experience notes that the fulfilment of national and regional commitments tends to be compliance reporting with a focus on local implementation of laws during public holidays around women.

Including gender on the global agenda

As a Human Resource practitioner, it is important to be "in the know". Part of your responsibility as an agent of change is to ensure that current trends and topical issues are used in your mainstreaming strategy. The onus is therefore on you to ensure that you are plugged into the forums that are in the public domain. The sub-section below looks at the work of corporates. However, in Chapter 4, when discussing collaborations, you will note the plethora of assistance available to you when developing and implementing your gender mainstreaming strategy.

In March 2019, Price Waterhouse Coopers teamed up with the UN Women's HeforShe Initiative towards achieving gender equality globally. Notably this did coincide with International Women's Day but allowed South Africa to be part of a global initiative aimed at changing mindsets. Price Waterhouse Coopers Global division is committed to also popularising their gains by launching "Bold Actions for Gender Equality" and challenging each international branch to highlight their achievements. Many branches have highlighted issues such as work/life balance, equal opportunities for women and celebrating female role models within its ranks.[84]

The South African arm of Price Waterhouse Coopers more specifically hosts the Gender Awards within the private and public sectors and therefore encourages public recognition of gender initiatives within and outside its sector. These interventions are, in my view, progressive in approach as they allow for collaboration and integration between the sectors. Notably, several categories are included such as Women on Boards, Equal Representation and Participation and Investing in Young Women, to name a few. It has been my experience that practices around youth development are relegated to internships and that often mentorship and coaching is not offered to women, with budgetary constraints being cited as the most common barrier to implementation. The importance of collaboration will be unpacked further in Chapter 4.

The World Bank is another example of private sector involvement in the furtherance of gender equality initiatives. The World Bank has launched a research series into the cost of gender inequality. These research reports are informative and seek to assist with mainstreaming initiatives by highlighting the losses incurred by gender inequality if not adequately addressed. This first note in the series on the cost of gender inequality focuses on the losses in national wealth due to gender inequality in earnings. The analyses presented in the report indicate the potential losses in Gross Domestic Product (GDP) from inequality between women and men in labour markets.[85] While the cost of gender inequality – in terms of human capital losses – for development is not solely due to losses in earnings, the impact of gender inequality on earnings is key. This is the area on which this note focuses.

The World Bank is often deferred to as the leader in economic measurement for countries. The World Bank therefore creates an enabling environment by its mere prioritisation of gender equality on the global agenda. The focus of research series such as these holds a mirror up to countries when considering the loss of earnings which is often the main bone of contention in the equality debates. "Equal work for equal pay" is the mantra that has come be to known for several decades; however, a research series such as this concretises this notion and provides a yardstick with which to count the cost thereof.

Chapter nine Institutions

Chapter nine institutions refer to a group of organisations established in terms of Chapter 9 of the South African Constitution to guard democracy. The institutions are[86]:

★ the Public Protector

★ the South African Human Rights Commission (SAHRC)

★ the Commission for the Promotion and Protection of the Rights of Cultural, Religious and Linguistic Communities (CRL Rights Commission)

★ the Commission for Gender Equality (CGE)

★ the Auditor-General

★ the Independent Electoral Commission (IEC)

★ the Independent Authority to Regulate Broadcasting

★ the Independent Communications Authority of South Africa (Icasa).

Of direct relevance to the gender mainstreaming debate is the Human Rights Commission and the Commission for Gender Equality.

According to the Research Brief on Gender and Equality in South Africa 2013–2017[87], the fact that women have historically been marginalised and regarded as unequal compared to men in terms of social and power relations has given rise to significant social, cultural and economic inequalities. Briefs such as these inform the current status quo and reflect women's unequal position within society. In terms of household income, it is noted and concerning that men earn almost twice what women earn on an annual basis.[88] Even though there are significant gains made in the South African economy, these analyses reveal that indeed women remain in a subordinate position to men.

The Commission for Gender Equality (CGE) is a major entity within the South African landscape responsible for gender equality in the country. The CGE is a constitutional entity, relied upon to 'strengthen constitutional democracy'.[89] Notably, the legal division of the Commission for Gender Equality provides direct services to the public by investigating gender-related complaints. Amongst other functions, the Commission for Gender Equality evaluates laws, customs, practices and Indigenous law, personal and family law affecting gender equality or status of women that are in force or proposed by Parliament.

The Chapter nine institutions provide resources and assistance to Human Resource practitioners in the struggle for gender equality and must be viewed as such. These institutions can provide guidance and assistance for sector-specific enquiries that may be otherwise unknown in the public domain.

This chapter provided an overview of country and private sector cases that are viewed as forerunners in the gender equality struggle. The cases are to be reflected upon for their significance to the South African experience. The Chapter nine institutions are discussed briefly above and serve as a resource to Human Resource practitioners across sectors. The next chapter unpacks the important role that senior management plays in creating an enabling environment and offers practical guidance as to how to hold senior management accountable for their commitments or lack thereof to gender equality in their institutions.

CHAPTER 4

Developing Senior Management Buy-In

As a Human Resource practitioner you will note that for any project to be successful, the buy-in from senior management is crucial. Gumede[90] claims that in post-Apartheid South Africa, "Significant challenges facing the democratic government included rebuilding the institutional mechanisms and initiating and implementing legislation and policies that are in line with the Constitution to usher in a new era of a developmental State." Gumede speaks to the important role of an enabling environment in facilitating the implementation of gender mainstreaming. This aspect is important to ensuring gender mainstreaming implementation in organisations across sectors.

Dan Gilmore, Editor-in-Chief of *Supply Chain Digest*, penned a piece headlined "What is Senior Management Support for Supply Chain Projects?" He noted that everyone says you need senior management support for a project to be successful, but no one really defines what it means. In fact, the phrase is used so gratuitously, in his opinion, to the point where it has become meaningless. He concludes that organisations need to define what senior management support really means.[91]

Sherry Gordan from Spendmatters offers some insight as to possible consequences, should you attempt to implement projects, especially around transformation, without senior management support:

★ The most common and show-stopping consequence is little or no budget allocated to do a particular project or initiative. If senior management doesn't truly support a particular initiative, they won't give sufficient, if any, money to do it. This will lessen the chances of project success or else prevent it from going forward altogether.

★ When things go wrong or you run into trouble, senior management won't interfere. If you go forward with a project or initiative that is unsupported, you're on your own when: people won't cooperate; people stonewall the implementation; people won't use a new system or process.

★ Forget getting cooperation from other functions. Sure, you can implement within the four walls of your function. But whoever implemented a successful supply management project, or for that matter, any significant initiative, that way? Most initiatives with any impact require cross-functional cooperation. It is much harder to get that cooperation without the bosses of other functions being on board. Senior management can enable that support.

★ Senior management wants and requires their goals and objectives to be implemented. If a supply management initiative doesn't support or clearly fit into senior management's goals and objectives, then they might fail to meet those goals because in their minds they are focusing on unrelated activities. Members of senior management do not want to miss their goals or they will be in trouble.

★ Change from the bottom up might be a way to get started, then try to gain senior management support based on the success of a grass-roots initiative. This might work in politics, but it doesn't translate very well to the business world. Bottom-up initiatives are uphill battles. They are time-consuming, difficult and fraught with peril. Initiatives started this way may initially enjoy some success, but they are hard to sustain and expand.

Heathfield[92] claims that successful change management requires a large commitment from executives and senior managers, whether the change is occurring in a department or in a complete organisation.

> "A change effort cannot be optional for senior staff. They must lead or get out of the way. The new system will ultimately have to stand on its own feet, but every new system needs support and nurture."[93]

As a Human Resource practitioner, leading what is essentially a transformation strategy, it is perhaps to be expected that there will be some resistance to change. Not all senior managers, who are expected to lead and implement from the top-down, will be in favour of gender equality. This is simply a reality.

Change Produces Anxiety and Uncertainty – Even Fear – in Employees
Employees may lose their sense of security. They may prefer the status quo. The range of reactions, when change is introduced, is unpredictable. No employee is left unaffected by most changes. As a result, resistance to change often occurs when change is introduced.

Change creates anxiety in organisations; this is a natural response. It is your responsibility to provide a safe environment where the message of gender equality and the prospect of implementing a gender equality strategy seems like a worthwhile exercise. This is built through the development of an employee culture through constant messaging. The latter is discussed in Chapter 9.

Balancecareers[94] offers some key advice on how to manage change effectively:

★ How much trust exists currently within your organisation? Is this enough trust?

★ Do you have a history of open communication and employee support for change efforts?

★ Do people feel positive about their work environment? Is your culture employee-friendly?

★ Do you share financial information? Is communication transparent?

★ Have you experienced a lot of changes and managed them successfully, so your employees are ready to change, and not change-weary?

★ Turn the change vision into an overall gender action plan and timeline, and plan to practise forgiveness when the timeline encounters barriers. Solicit input to the plan from people who own or work on the processes that are changing. Otherwise, you will set your organisation up for unwanted and unnecessary resistance.

★ Gather information about and determine ways to communicate the reasons for the changes. These may include the changing economic environment, changing competitive environment, customer needs and expectations, vendor capabilities, government regulations, population demographics, financial considerations, resource availability, and company direction.

★ Assess each potential impact to organisation processes, systems, customers, and staff. Assess the risks and have a particular improvement or mitigation plan developed for each risk.

★ Plan the communication of the change. People have to understand the context, the reasons for the change, the plan and the organisation's clear expectations for their new roles and responsibilities. Nothing communicates expectations better than improved measurements and rewards and recognition.

★ Determine the WIIFM (what's in it for me) of the change for each person in your organisation. Work on how the change will affect each employee directly, and how to make the change fit his or her needs as well as those of the organisation.

The enabling environment is inextricably linked to the overriding factor of political will. Without the political will and buy-in from key role-players, both internal and external to the Department, the success of the gender projects is ultimately unachievable. Brynard,[95] in his assessment of the various factors that influence policy development, claims that the organisational environment plays a critical role in the implementation of policy. How then do you attain buy-in from senior management?

Let's look at what senior managers are expected to do.

Core responsibilities of the senior manager include:

★ Providing guidance to direct reports, typically comprising first-line managers and supervisors.

★ Ensuring clarity around priorities and goals for the entire functional area.

★ Approving requests for investment to a certain level of authority.

★ Managing overall financial budgeting for her function.

★ Approving hiring and firing requests within her group.

★ Guiding the talent identification and development processes for a group or function.

★ Working across functions with peers in other groups to ensure collaboration for shared goals

★ Interacting with senior management for reporting.

★ Working with senior management and other peers for strategy development and execution planning.

★ Communicating financial and goal results and key performance indicators to direct reports.

★ Facilitating goal-level creation for the broader function and working with managers to ensure the goals cascade to all workers.

Consider the information box below – this makes a short case for the employment of senior managers. These positions are not always needed in a large number due to the core business of the organisation and are often linked to budgets available for the skills level required. Complexity and inefficiency tend to increase as organisations grow and become more stratified with additional layers of management.

Why Employ This Position?

It's common for larger firms to evaluate their positions by scope, responsibility, size, and budgetary authority, and then to assign a level to these positions. The senior manager level or designation represents a step up from the manager and offers the opportunity for individuals to take on new responsibilities and increase their contributions.

Performance Management

Performance Management is perhaps one of the most common approaches for ensuring gender mainstreaming in an organisation. As a Human Resource practitioner, performance management is one of the core duties one has to undertake. It is important however to attain senior management buy-in order to mainstream the relevant performance indicators to ensure that gender mainstreaming occurs at all levels of an organisation. Notably, senior management buy-in may be difficult to ascertain. However, the development of a Gender Management Committee at your organisation with key representatives at all levels, will assist in circumventing this. This committee should be representative of employees at all levels with a specific focus on the inclusion of men. This is to ensure that gender is not relegated to being a women's issue and to ensure a fair representation of interests. This committee should be led by the highest office, namely the Chief Executive Office or Head of Department. The committee's duties include but are not limited to the overall management of interventions to assist with the mainstreaming of gender for gender equality at your organisation. The proposals emanating from this committee must be presented at the Executive Management meetings to ensure that buy-in is received from the highest level.

Below is the 8 Point Principle Plan, provided to Heads of Department within the State to ensure that gender is mainstreamed. It must be noted that these principles are not mandated to appear in performance agreements. However, it is my view that these principles be mainstreamed into all positions of leadership across sectors to ensure a more equitable workplace.

The 8 Principles are the following[96]:

1. Transformation for non-sexism.
2. Establishing a policy environment.
3. Meeting equity targets.
4. Creating an enabling environment.
5. Gender mainstreaming.
6. Empowerment.

7. Provide adequate resources.

8. Accountability, Monitoring and Evaluation.

These principles can be mainstreamed into the performance agreements of an entire organisation in order to hold people accountable to the ultimate goal of gender equality. Notably, formal policies on gender equality and a gender action plan must be developed for an organisation holistically. However, the development of such policies and action plans cannot precede the formal buy-in from senior management who are responsible for the creation of an enabling environment.

Senior managers, by virtue of their titles, are not immune to failing. Many lead and manage interchangeably and therefore need support and capacity building. Consider the following quote from Leadership Watch:

> Funnily enough, senior leaders are often not aware of their changing role. They tend to see their role in defining the strategy and priorities, in clarifying the decisions taken, but for the execution they expect their line management to take over. And maybe that is exactly why companies today are struggling with change fatigue? Maybe senior leaders expect too much from line managers as the key responsible for the execution of change? Maybe they underestimate the fact that leading change today requires a different relationship between senior and middle management?[97]

What can be done to alleviate this pressure? Senior leaders need to be close to their management. Close in terms of explaining the change, discussing potential ways to manage it successfully, initiating the right focus and right actions, guiding the desired behaviour and results. Create a direct link with your management teams and keep up a high level of openness and frequent communication.

What You Should Expect from Senior Leaders During Change[98]

Senior leaders can do the following to lead effectively during successful change management efforts.

★ Establish a clear vision for the change management process. Paint a picture of where the organisation will end up and the anticipated outcomes. Make certain the picture is one of reality and not what people wish would occur. When this vision and communication is done well, each employee should be able to describe what he or she will experience on the other side of making the change. For employees, the most significant factor is the impact of the change in their job. This is an often neglected step.

★ Appoint an executive champion who owns the change management process and makes certain other senior managers, as well as other appropriate people in the organisation, are involved. Change is easier when a large number of people who must change are involved in the planning and implementation.

★ Pay attention to the changes occurring. Ask employees how things are going. Focus on progress and barriers to change management. One of the worst possible scenarios is to have the leaders ignore the process.

★ Sponsor portions of the change or the change management process, as an involved participant, to increase active involvement and interaction with other organisation members.

★ If personal or managerial actions or behaviours require change for the changes to take hold in the organisation, model the new behaviours and actions. Walk the talk. Senior leaders play a huge role in teaching their reporting staff expected and desired behaviour.

★ Establish a structure which will support the change. This may take the form of a Steering Committee, Leadership Group, or Guiding Coalition.

★ Change the measurement, reward, and recognition systems to measure and reward the accomplishment of the new expectations. Make the recognition public so that you reinforce the behaviours that you really want to see with all of your other employees.

★ Solicit and act upon feedback from other members of the organisation. What's working? Not working? How can you improve the processes? When you act on feedback or decide not to, make sure you have let the employee with the idea know what you did or why not.

★ Recognise the human element in the change. People have different needs and different ways of reacting to change. They need time to deal with and adjust to change.

★ Senior leaders must participate in the training that other organisation members attend, but, even more importantly, they must exhibit their "learning" from the sessions, readings, interactions, tapes, books or research.

★ Be honest and worthy of trust. Treat people with the same respect that you expect from them. Change is difficult and progresses when the people involved feel supported, respected, and that you care about them.

Setting targets

Setting targets for gender equality in the workplace is a difficult exercise and requires much negotiation and influence. Targets are achievable, time-framed objectives which organisations can set on a regular basis to focus their efforts on achieving improved outcomes. They are an essential part of managing business performance and most organisations are familiar with a target-setting process for financial and operating performance. Gender targets operate in much the same way by setting objectives around a key management area of focus, in this case, gender composition.[99]

Key principles of target setting:

★ Clarity: Set clear targets with time-lines to ensure progress can be measured.

★ Small steps: Consider setting interim goals and measures as steps towards a longer-term goal. This will focus immediate efforts and encourage momentum, while enabling the organisation to monitor progress.

★ Control: Ensure managers are able to influence the metrics and have appropriate control over the strategies and initiatives to achieve the targets.

★ Realistic: Set targets that can be achieved. This requires a thorough analysis of all of the possible barriers to achieving targets and the support needed for maximising the opportunities to achieve them.

★ **Accountability:** Create managerial accountabilities and rewards, e.g. linking remuneration or career progression to achieving targets.

Consider the Workplace Gender Equality Agency's benchmarks being implemented in Australia:

> The Workplace Gender Equality Agency develops industry-specific educational benchmarks relating to gender, including benchmarks related to gender composition of the workforce. This will allow organisations to compare themselves to their industry peers and track their progress over time. While there is no requirement to set gender targets under the Workplace Gender Equality Act 2012, an organisation that does so will likely improve its performance relative to the benchmarks and have better access to the entire talent pool.

Consider the use of the following checklist when looking at inserting the relevant performance targets related to gender equality[100]:

Table 4.1: Developing a strategy for high-level implementation

Theme	Action	Present/Absent
Leadership commitment	There is overt commitment to gender equality at all levels of management, including at the CEO and executive management level.	
Strategic intent	Gender equality, and diversity more generally, are accepted as business imperatives (e.g. in the same way as safety).	
	There is a gender equality strategy, plan or set of objectives that are clearly aligned or integrated with the overall business strategy and planning processes (e.g. in terms of priority and resourcing).	

Theme	Action	Present/Absent
Stakeholder management	There are strategies for communicating internally and externally the organisation's targets, its commitment to the targets, and its approach in determining the targets.	
	Key internal stakeholders (e.g. those with responsibility for talent management) are engaged directly with the target-setting process.	
Accountability	The organisation has clearly identifiable accountabilities for the delivery of gender equality outcomes and to meeting agreed gender targets.	
Measurement and reporting	The organisation has measurement and reporting systems in place to both monitor progress and evaluate the impact of changes made.	
	The organisation will make a public commitment to gender targets and report publicly (e.g. via its annual report) on progress made towards meeting the targets including the strategies implemented to increase gender equality and the impact of these strategies on attitudes, culture and performance.	
	There is commitment to embed gender targets into business unit goals and sharing experience across departmental heads.	

Theme	Action	Present/Absent
Organisational culture and systems	The organisation has reviewed, and where necessary amended, policies and processes to encourage gender equality, including those relating to: recruitment and selection, performance management, pay and remuneration, training and development, talent identification, leadership capability models and career structures.	

Clarify assumptions

Consider the following factors that influence how targets are set:

★ Expectations about the size of your organisation in the future, both in terms of possible growth or contraction.

★ Likely exits from positions relevant to your target group.

★ Possible scenarios for restructuring and changes in the number of positions within the target group.

★ Specific interventions already planned that could have an impact on your target-setting process (e.g. a planned strategy to target the recruitment of women into non- traditional roles).

Values Based Leadership (VBL)

The buy-in from senior management is inextricably linked to their values. How will you drum up political will for a pertinent marginalised issue such as gender equality if your senior management cohort does not value this? Values Based Leadership (VBL) is therefore an area to be explored in attempting to mainstream gender for gender equality. Whilst it is important to note that management and leadership are definitely separate as theories, in a transformational process it is important to position leaders and mainstream the values of an organisation.

> Steve Jobs said,
> "The only thing that works is management by values."

It's no surprise that companies like Apple, who foster a values-based approach in their leadership culture, create connections that have a significant impact on company performance.[101] *The Financial Times* defines value-based leadership as "Motivating employees by connecting organizational goals to employees' personal values." Often there is a misalignment between personal values and organisational values. Notably, these have to be aligned in a creative way through shifting mindsets. There are many elements that make us view the world in different ways – our age, race, education, geographical location, religion, to name a few. These elements ultimately make us diverse. However, gender equality is not a "nice to have" or "events exercise". This is a legislated requirement and must be adhered to if we are to live in a transformed society.

A Harvard Business School Paper[102] asserted that when leaders focus on the technical or administrative side of their work, they become too fixed on short-term returns. The paper stated, "If leaders instead sought to uphold values and maintain integrity, they could establish the long-term perspective and commitment to innovation necessary for sustaining their competitive position in an increasingly global economy." Part of this integrity is the commitment to gender equality in the workplace. Values-based leaders are those with an underlying moral, ethical foundation. VBL describes behaviours that are rooted in ethical and moral foundations. Examples of prominent VBL styles in leadership research include spiritual, servant, authentic, ethical and transformational leadership.

Speaking to values-based leadership, Mark Fernandes, Chief Leadership Officer at Luck Companies, says: "In order for these values to be authentic within the organization, it's imperative that the leaders be fully committed to demonstrating the values in everything they do. There's a level of inauthenticity that associates will notice and it can erode their trust in the leadership if they're not actively seeing the behaviors exhibited in the actions and words of their leaders."

The values ascribed to for gender equality cannot be simply stated in a vision and mission poster in your organisation. In order to make this real, management and those who have a position of influence in your organisation must reflect on the following questions[103]:

> "How can I integrate our core organisational values into the way my team operates?"

> "What are some ways I can communicate our values to my team over the next thirty days?"

> "How can I create greater personal alignment with our values on a daily basis?"

> "How can I recognise and reward people who actively embody the values?"

Freifeld[104] claims that in order to build a values-based organisation, one has to extend trust from the middle. Whilst gender mainstreaming is a top-down strategy as discussed earlier, the implementation thereof is ultimately a transformation strategy led by management. As a Human Resource practitioner, you need to understand the role of trust building in developing a gender mainstreaming strategy for gender equality. Transformation is not a paper exercise and is therefore written with the understanding that employees need to embody the values of the organisation. Managers are in a unique position to provide leadership by embodying and implementing the value of gender equality in the workplace.

Hames[105] explains several steps that can be implemented in looking at how to approach values-based leadership in managing gender mainstreaming as a strategy for gender equality. Look at how you can inspire managers to "Walk the Values". Design a culture initiative that empowers managers to act as culture exemplars and ethics envoys to their teams. This will promote a stronger ethical culture and breed greater trust amongst their teams. Research shows that a manager's consistency in word and deed sets the tone. When managers are not involved and do not serve on the front line as culture envoys, it can breed a tone of cynicism and scepticism among their employees.

Create a shared vision[106], create a campaign and kick it off with a visible launch with senior leaders and middle managers present. (Campaigns are discussed in more detail in Chapter 9). The objective is to inspire middle management with a compelling vision of how culture matters, and how leadership on the front line shapes culture. In practice at the local level, invite managers to embrace and cascade the values message by sharing stories of when the company and its people really "walked the walk" on mission and values. The latter must be carefully managed so as not to intimidate the current employees. The use of case studies as presentations can also assist with this and is unpacked extensively in Chapter 8.

Toolkits and coaching can assist with embedding the shared vision. Managers at every level need the right tools to engage their teams on the company's values and expected behaviours. Managers should be encouraged to have regular discussions with their teams to keep values on everyone's minds. Managers will need coaching on how to comfortably conduct values discussions with their teams. Research suggests that discussion-based training that explores challenging, grey-area situations may have the most impact. Many organisations are developing toolkits – electronic versions of "meetings in a box" – that contain resources, case studies, facilitator guides, and other learning aids to help bring values to life. Be prepared to refresh and revise the case discussions to stay on top of the relevant issues and keep employees engaged. Consider collecting real stories from employee participants to enrich the case discussion. Case studies are discussed in Chapter 8.

These initiatives cannot be undertaken unless they have a performance management component that concretises commitments to gender equality. Poor performance against targets must be addressed and recognition must be offered to those who are able to reflect their commitment to gender equality through their outputs. In high-performing cultures, recognition and celebration can reinforce the spirit of the company. Promoting greater alignment between the company's core values and day-to-day operations through real stories helps crystallise the message to employees worldwide. Identify communication channels and forums to publicly celebrate employees for their acts of values-based leadership and values-based decision making.

Vinamaki[107] identifies five critical success factors for the implementation of a values-based leadership as a strategy towards achieving gender equality in the workplace. She explains that organisations have to look at the major changes in how people related in the 21st Century when approaching values-based leadership.

1. Traditional power is becoming powerless in flat and professional organisations.

2. The participation of stakeholders is suggested to be intensive and extensive.

3. New forms of control and feedback are needed.

4. The communication of values should be clear and straightforward.

5. Leadership stands for fostering a good image and perceptions.

These elements are unpacked in later chapters and will inform you on how to implement gender mainstreaming as a transformation strategy towards gender equality. "Balance Careers" advocate that the development of values must be understood and implemented in order for this to be communicated well.

To identify organisation values, bring together your executive group to:

★ Learn about and discuss the power of shared values.

★ Obtain consensus that these leaders are committed to creating a values-based workplace.

★ Define the role of the executives in leading this process.

★ Provide written material the executives can share with their reporting staff.

Design and schedule a series of values alignment sessions in which all members of the organisation will participate. Schedule each member of the organisation to attend a three- to four-hour session. (If your group is small, it is most effective for all members to meet in one session together.)

These sessions are most effective when led by a trained facilitator. This allows each member of your organisation to fully participate in the process. Alternatively, train internal facilitators who lead one session, and participate in another. The session must be preceded by some activities that participants must undertake as part of their fulfilment of the requirements of attendance. Each person brings his or her own set of values to the workplace. Sharing similar or agreed-upon values at work helps clarify: expected behaviour and actions towards each other and customers, how decisions are made, and exactly what is important in the organisation. This exercise also seeks to build trust. Employees must be carefully managed in the sessions in order to create common values. The latter will result in the development of value statements:

Examples of Value Statements:[108]

Integrity:

We maintain credibility by making certain our actions always match our words and uphold the notion that men and women are equal.

Respect:

We respect each person's right to be involved, to the greatest extent possible or desired, in making informed decisions about his or her core functions.

Accountability:

We accept personal responsibility to efficiently use organization resources, improve our systems, and help others improve their effectiveness.

The values are not however just written up and left to the employee to fulfil. You will have to institute a follow-up process to try to embed these values in the psyche of the employee.

In an article entitled the "Value of Values Clarification – Just Stop That Navel Gazing", Robert Bacal, a Canadian writer and consultant, offers these cautions:

★ "Don't oversell the process.

★ Always anchor, or relate the values expressed to real-world problems.

★ Encourage people to identify examples where there is a gap between values, or beliefs, and behavior.

★ Remember that you are not going to alter a person's values and beliefs by talking about them. Values clarification exercises are, at best, an opportunity to share them, not change them."

If you want your investment in this workplace values identification and alignment process to make a difference in your organisation, the leadership, and individual follow-up is critical. The organisation must commit to change and enhance work behaviours, actions and interactions. Reward and recognition systems and performance management systems must support and reward new behaviours. Consequences must exist for behaviours that undermine the values agreed upon.

CHAPTER 5

Nurturing a Supportive Community

Mainstreaming gender as a strategy for gender equality can be a lonely road. It is therefore imperative that you, as a Human Resource practitioner, collaborate with key role players within your organisation. Some of these role players have been alluded to earlier, namely senior management and those identified to be on the Gender Management Committee. These relationships and collaborative methods must be developed over time with enough efforts from you as the Human Resource practitioner responsible for gender mainstreaming. There is also a need to collaborate with organisations outside of yours as many are working in the gender landscape and can be of great assistance.

Let's take a look at building a supportive employee work culture for gender equality. This is no easy feat as the South African context provides for a cultural mix that often rejects gender equality as a valid claim in the workplace.

> Companies should develop clear guidelines for what collegial and respectful behaviour looks like—as well as unacceptable and uncivil behaviour. To be treated seriously, these guidelines must be supported by a clear reporting process and swift consequences for disrespectful behaviour. Companies should also hold periodic refreshers to drive the guidelines home and make sure all employees understand them. Steps like these have an impact on employee satisfaction and retention. Both women and men who believe that disrespectful behaviour toward women is often quickly addressed at their company are happier in their roles and less likely to think about leaving.[109]

Importantly, you must recognise the role of men as agents of change. Men can and should advocate for gender equality and provide leadership in their frame of reference (meaning not only senior managers). This means that Human Resources needs to look at who the progressive men are in your organisation who may already subscribe to the notion of gender equality and start by using these employees as agents of change, to "get the message out". This leads to building a supportive community internally.

Mike Gamson, Senior Vice President for LinkedIn Global Solutions.[110]

Gamson shares the wisdom that led him to make significant progress toward gender equality at LinkedIn, acknowledging three things that men in leadership positions can do:

1. Recognise the unconscious biases that are maintaining the status quo and disadvantage other groups.

2. Focus on recruitment and hiring. Gamson advocates for a highly deliberate emphasis on creating a diverse workforce.

3. Invest in high-potential employees and set aside investments that are explicitly there to reach underrepresented talent.

The increased number of women in the workplace is not an end in itself. This must be addressed through looking at practical ways of retaining women in the workplace and advancing women from junior and middle positions to positions of seniority. Champion less, listen more, advocate most: It can get paradoxical when men start to assert themselves in the workplace to create a more welcoming environment for women. Support women in leadership and emerging leadership roles and challenge them, in turn, to spearhead efforts to improve gender equality in the workforce.

A supportive organisational culture fosters a better working environment and ultimately productivity rises. Creating a supportive workplace culture takes time and requires multiple and mutually reinforcing strategies. Three critical strategies that underpin workplace culture change work are[111]:

★ Involving workers.

★ Engaging leaders.

★ involving women and men.

Commission for Gender Equality

The Commission for Gender Equality has already been mentioned in Chapter 1 and has been explained at length. This organisation is a key Chapter nine institution that can assist with providing guidance with regard to complaints received. Their legal division in particular advises parliament on legislation and also undertakes cases. However, there are many other organisations that can aid and guide you on the path towards gender equality in your workplace.

Noteworthy cases defended by the Commission for Gender Equality:

> M v S, 2016 Mbombela Magistrates Court (Equality Court)
>
> The CGE Mpumalanga received a complaint in December 2016. The complaint relates to the unfair gender discrimination of the complainant who was employed as a security guard at "S", Nelspruit. The complainant was designated to work at "S", Nelspruit. On or about the 10th November 2016, the complainant was informed by the manager of "S" that she is no longer wanted as an employee because she is a lesbian. The manager of "S" allegedly indicated that the complainant is allowed to be lesbian outside the workplace but in the workplace, it's not allowed. Subsequent to this a notice to staff members was put at the staff entrance. Point 5 of the notice read that "gay lady to be replaced not allowed to search ladies". According to the complainant this notice was also visible to the members of the public and consequently led to her humiliation. The complainant was thus dismissed at work and is currently unemployed.
>
> The conduct of "S" amounted to unfair gender discrimination and humiliation. The complainant in this matter sought damages of R120 000,00 and an apology. The CGE brought the matter before the equality court. The matter was settled out of court and the complainant was reinstated and received three months of salary. The perpetrator was subjected to a disciplinary hearing and further attended an awareness workshop on human rights.[112]

This case demonstrates the need to adhere to the legislation outlined earlier. Where employers discriminate on the basis of sexual orientation, recourse can and should be sourced in the pursuit of gender justice. Complaints do not only emanate from employees, complaints about company/State departmental practices can also emanate from those who are not employed by that particular institution as evidenced below:

> Raedani v M and others 2016 case no 1/2016 Thohoyandou Magistrates Court (Equality Court)

> The CGE received this complaint on the 13th October 2016. The complaint relates to an interview conducted at University of Venda Radio Station on the 19th September 2016 wherein the first respondent said: "I talked to one boy who is gay, I told him to change his thinking (being gay) because the backdoor (anus) is not meant for sex, but it is meant for waste removal (going to toilet) ... a lot of them are HIV Positive ... a person has a chance to change and repent from deeds that are not good, a man will tell himself (realise) that he is a man and not a woman, and a woman also realise that she is woman and not a man and live (enter) a good life".

> The respondent allegedly stated further that "in the programmes that I run at the NGO, I am allowed to employ/hire gays, lesbians, sex workers and people think I like it (i.e employing gays, lesbians & sex workers) but that is not the case, it is my way of getting an opportunity/chance to talk to them and convince them to change ... many have changed (from their Gays'/Lesbians' ways) ... When you want to change them you do not go around chasing after them, you must just get close to them ... if you want to catch a chicken, you throw a mealie-meal so as the chicken can come next to you, that is when you catch it".

> The above remarks amount to hate speech and are thus discriminatory and further perpetuate violence towards the LGBTI persons. The complainant in this matter sought damages of R50 000,00 and an apology. The CGE was admitted as *amicus curiae* in this matter. The matter is still pending before the Thohoyandou Magistrates Court.[113]

Finally, another noteworthy case is that of the issue of discrimination towards the spouses of employees when administering benefits. A landmark case has influenced how employers may treat those in the LGBTI community:

> National Coalition for Gay and Lesbian Equality and Others v Minister of Home Affairs and Others

80

The National Coalition for Gay and Lesbian Equality (NCGLE), joined by six same sex couples and the Commission for Gender Equality (CGE), brought an application in the Cape Provincial Division of the High Court against the Minister, Deputy Minister and Director General of Home Affairs. The case was then referred to the Constitutional Court.

The CGE was the fourteenth applicant in this matter.

This case raised two important questions:

1. Whether it is constitutional for immigration law to facilitate the immigration into South Africa of the spouses of permanent South African residents but not to afford the same benefits to gays and lesbians in permanent same sex life partnerships with permanent South African residents;

2. Whether when it concludes that provisions in a statute are unconstitutional, the court may read words into the statute to remedy the unconstitutionality. These questions arise from the provisions of section 25(5) of the Aliens Control Act 96 of 1991 and the applications of the provisions of section 172(1)(b) of the 1996 Constitution should section 25(5) be found to be inconsistent with the Constitution.

Section 25(5) essentially discriminated on the basis of sexual orientation and therefore violated the constitutional right to equality in that it omitted to give persons who are partners in permanent same sex life partnerships the benefits it extends to spouses.

The court found that Section 25(5) reinforced harmful stereotypes of gays and lesbians and it essentially conveys the message that gays and lesbians lack the inherent humanity to have their families and family lives respected or protected. It was held that the section discriminated unfairly against gays and lesbians on the grounds of sexual orientation and marital status and limited their equality rights and right to dignity. The limitation was found to be unreasonable and unjustifiable in an open and democratic society based on human dignity, equality and freedom.

The decision in the National Coalition case paved the way for the realisation of rights for same sex couples in that subsequent judgments extended other benefits of marriage to same sex couples, including adoption, medical and pension benefits, etc. In December 2005, the Constitutional Court ruled, in Minister of Home Affairs v Fourie that marriage should be extended to same sex couples. This was duly done with the passage of the Civil Union Act No. 17 of 2006.[114]

This landmark case has paved the way in which the employer has to also treat beneficiaries of employee's benefits. The cases above are of value and must be reflected upon to inform current practices at your organisation.

Sector Education Training Authorities

I now turn your attention to a major element of gender mainstreaming – that of capacity building. Many employees claim that they do not mainstream gender as they do not know how to accomplish this in their work. In Chapter 2, the issue of performance agreements was raised as a major tool to ensure mainstreaming into operations. The skills associated with the delivery thereof lie in the Gender Action Plan that you and your senior management team will develop for your organisation. Part of the needs will be to upskill and/or reskill employees on how to mainstream gender. You must look at available budgets for such skills interventions and this element can be a major constraint for the implementation of your Gender Action Plan.

It is important to be aware of the Skills Levy available in South Africa and access thereof. All organisations with a payroll of more than R500k per annum are required to pay a Skills Development Levy of 1% of that payroll. Your organisation is able to claim up to 50% of these fees back. You will need to register with your particular Sector Education and Training Authority (SETA). You then need to decide what training would strategically benefit your organisation and your employees best (taking into account factors such as company growth strategies, succession planning, BEE Scorecards, management grooming, upliftment programmes, employees' career development and skill needs, etc). As part of your general duties as a Human Resource practitioner, you will need to put together a training plan for the year. In order to access the funds available, you must compile and submit a Workplace Skills Plan to your SETA (the template for the Workplace Skills Plan is on your SETA's website or you can often submit it online). The SETA training year runs from 1 April each year until 31 March the following year –

the Workplace Skills Plans needs to be submitted by 30 June. It is important to also check these websites regularly as funded programmes are often made available to all sectors. This will enable you to fulfil not just commitments to training on gender mainstreaming, but the fulfilment of additional skills obligations as reflected in your Workplace Skills Plan.

National Gender Machinery

The South African State has developed a set of structures that are required to mainstream gender as a strategy for gender equality. The South African State is described as:

> The set of structures and processes (including the public service, the nature of governmental-social relationships and internal organisational dynamics) which evolve over time as a permanent part of the dynamics of government.[115]

The development and launch of the National Gender Machinery (NGM) was led by the then Office on the Status of Women (OSW) in the Presidency, which was responsible for the support of gender mainstreaming initiatives in the South African public service. The African Development Bank describes the National Gender Machinery, as follows:

> The Department of Women at the national level and in the Office of the Premiers at the provincial level. The Gender Focal Units or Points in government departments also exist at both national and provincial level and are coordinated by OSW.

> The CGE is an independent body and also has provincial offices.

> Finally, gender focused NGOs are also seen as forming part of the NGM.

The development of the National Gender Machinery was the result of much lobbying from the women's movement in South Africa. Sadly, many have become disillusioned with the National Gender Machinery as its efficacy is often questioned. The National Gender Machinery is meant to be driven by the Department of Women. The fact that this was tabled and passed in parliament as a new Ministry with a dedicated Department and not just a subsidiary unit under the Presidency as it was previously housed, shows

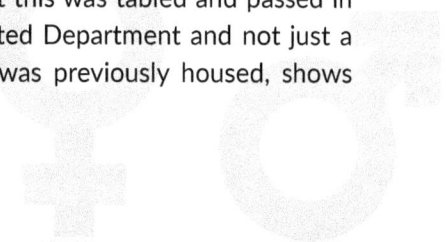

that gender was being elevated in 2009. Notably, this was driven under a Presidency that highlighted the aspect of gender equality in the manifesto of the ruling party, the African National Congress (ANC) and also gazetted the requirement for gender equity targets, thus formally reflecting the political will of politicians for the inclusion of gender equality. The formation of the Ministry was in my opinion a major step forward, however flawed the process may have been. The intent was to create a Ministry dedicated to gender issues along with those marginalised issues affecting people living with disabilities and the rights of children. The Ministry faced many obstacles at the start and struggled with the structure and appointment of skilled staff.

Efforts as recent as 2018 reflect that the Ministry is undertaking efforts to revive the National Gender Machinery. Organisations are welcome to approach the Ministry to become part of this body and therefore this will ensure that you, as a Human Resource practitioner are plugged into the current developments within the State and have access to possible opportunities that may be availed for your organisation. If you are squarely based in the private sector, nothing prevents you from collaborating with non-government institutions who are working in the gender arena. A comprehensive list is available from the South African NGO Coalition.

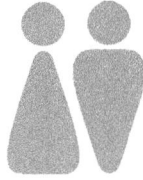

CHAPTER 6

Setting the rules

As a point of departure, "policy" as a concept must be unpacked. Fox and Meyer[116] explain that policy is "authoritative Statements made by legitimate public institutions about the way in which they propose to deal with policy problems". Anderson[117], defines policy as:

> ... a proposed course of action of a person, group, or government within a given environment providing obstacles and opportunities which the policy was proposed to utilise and overcome in an effort to reach a goal or realise an objective.

It is fundamentally important for organisations to develop policy. An organisation without policy is an organisation without control. If there were no formal documented policies, then organisation personnel at any level would have no guidance on how to make decisions.[118] Some of the benefits of formal policies include:

★ Helping staff to make decisions more efficiently.

★ Providing instruction on how to do tasks.

★ Creating confidence and reducing bias in decision-making

★ Protecting staff from acting in a manner that might endanger their employment.

★ Protecting staff from acting in a manner that might endanger the safety of themselves and others.

★ Helping staff to initiate actions and take responsibility without constant reference to management.

★ Increasing the accountability of business or organisations and their staff.

Consider the case of Mexico in the implementation of gender policy[119]:

In Mexico, a Gender Equity Model or "GEM 2003" was developed and tested by 57 firms with around 250,000 employees, and they were certified by the project closing date of December 2005. The model that was developed proved to be a successful tool for promoting gender equity in the private sector. The following were the empirical results that GEM 2003 identified in a qualitative survey administered to firms. The firms reported:

★ improved labor environment within the firm (31 percent of the firms)

★ better communication between management and workers (23 percent of the firms)

★ an increased number of women in managerial positions (9 percent of the firms)

★ increased productivity (8 percent of the firms)

★ reduction in salary gap (8 percent of the firms)

★ reduction in maternity-related discrimination (8 percent of the firms)

The dominant view on policy development is rooted in the New Management Paradigm (NPM). In South Africa the gender equality journey is dominated by public sector legislation and led by a culture of "customer care". NPM is identified with a technicist approach. The main criticism of the technicisit approach is that it loses the humanity of policy implementation and does not identify the actual citizen in a democracy.[120] In order to mainstream gender effectively, you must identify the receivers of policy as humans who have their own belief set that perhaps needs to be altered to find a balanced view of gender equality and elicit commitment from employees.

The dominant view on policy development is rooted in the New Management Paradigm (NPM). This school of thought emphasises policy as "a purposive course of action followed by an actor or set of actors".[121] It can be argued[122] that there are certain "unequivocal characteristics" of the NPM. This includes the concept of the customer and contracting. The South African policy discourse features all of these characteristics. For example, Batho Pele "People First", the White Paper on Transforming Public Service Delivery (1997), emphasises a "culture of customer care" and the adoption of the tools of the "new public service management".

Further to the dominant view of policy development, Boyte[123] advises that, "when politics becomes the property of professional elites, bureaucrats and consultants, most people are marginalised in the serious work of public affairs. Citizens are reduced to, at most, secondary roles as demanding consumers or altruistic volunteers". White emphasises that "democratic citizenship is undermined if there is too great a contradiction between the egalitarian norms of a democratic polity and the inequalities of individuals and groups in civil society".[124] Your main role as an advocator of gender equality in the workplace is to ensure that employees are not reduced to a secondary consumer of policy. You have to use campaigns and performance agreements as discussed in later chapters to foster support from the individual. Therefore, the individual becomes a self-motivator for gender equality initatives in the workplace.

Whilst South Africa has progressive policies and a Constitution that propagates gender equality, the realising of these paper rights is achieved in a very limited manner.[125] In trying to answer the question of the gap between policy and practice, Brynard[126] states:

"The policy gap is what transpires in the implementation process between policy expectations and perceived policy results". These paper rights become real when individuals take responsibility for the implementation of gender equality initiatives beyond compliance reporting around equity of numbers. The operationalising of gender mainstreaming therefore moves into the personal realm.

He argues that policy gaps are attributed to the absence of political commitment and policy-makers having too ambitious targets. In addition, and as is the case with the South African State, many international and regional obligations are drafted by other countries and are far removed from the operational level at which implementers are placed. It is envisaged that

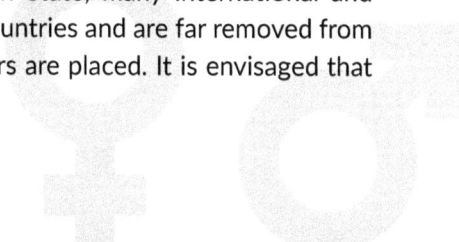

the gap between policy and implementation will be fulfilled through the formulation and adoption of the Gender Action Plan at your organisation. This plan will assist in the operationalising of gender mainstreaming activities.

The National Policy Framework for Women's Empowerment and Gender Equality is the overarching gender policy for the State as a whole. South Africa's National Policy Framework for Women's Empowerment and Gender Equality (2002), then known as the NPF and now known as the Gender Policy Framework, reflects the State's goal to attain gender equality. The policy details gender mainstreaming strategy imperatives and outlines long-term and short-term goals for the attainment of equal rights regardless of gender. Gender equity refers to the achievement of results that comply with the needs of both men and women. Gender equity strategies are employed to attain gender equality. Equality is achieved through using equity as a means.[127]

The Gender Policy Framework details tools for the achievement of gender equality. The review of existing policies and implementation of departmental action plans are squarely placed in the hands of provincial and national "GFPs". The policy assumes that each Gender Focal Point (GFP) is placed at a level that allows for impact and access to resources and also possesses the requisite skills for the development of departmental action plans. Key partners include Premiers, Ministers, Members of the Executive Council (MECs), Directors-General, the then OSW, and several Sector-Specific Organisations (CSOs).[128] There is a notable reliance on senior political officials to push the "gender agenda". It can be deduced that the GPF, through the naming of key partners, acknowledges the significance of political heads and administrative heads in the implementation of gender projects. The document speaks broadly of "women's organisations and sector specific civil society" but clearly notes the link of the public service to other sectors. Again, it is noted that without the political will of role-players, both internally and externally, the success of initiatives cannot be realised.

Tools emanating from the National Policy Framework[129] can be adapted for any sector. An adaptation of the tool on mainstreaming gender into projects follows:

Table 6.1: Mainstreaming gender into projects

Project Lifecycle	Phases in Gender Planning	Activities	Outputs
Conceptualisation	Situational Analysis; Review of current policies programmes; and budgets; Problem Identification	Assess inclusion of gender considerations into budgets, policies, programmes and practices	Common understanding regarding gender gaps, constraints and challenges
Project Planning	Develop gender-specific goals and priorities; Define strategic options	Consultations with Human Resources and Finance divisions Definition of target groups; Identification of gender objectives; Gender needs assessment	Methods for addressing gender gaps; Plans for gender budgets for departments
Project Design	Make strategic choices	Undertake strategic planning; Conduct internal consultations	Strategic objectives for addressing needs; Gender targets for programme delivery
	Appraisal	Gender training of staff in the project; Inclusion of gender advisory skills	Curriculum Gender specialists' job descriptions
	Ratification	Review of projects; Appraisal of gender component	Multi-disciplinary review of engendered projects; Requests for integration of gender

Project Lifecycle	Phases in Gender Planning	Activities	Outputs
Project Implementation	Prepare the organisation for action	Undertake an educational programme	Gender sensitisation programme; Policies for institutionalising gender equality; Development and enhancement of Management Information System
Project Evaluation	Undertake regular evaluation	Conduct consultations; Review written reports	Project appraisal report

(Adapted from: South Africa's National Policy Framework for Women's Empowerment and Gender Equality)[130]

These plans cannot be realised without the prerequisite set of skills needed to implement the projects that will ultimately lead to the success of gender mainstreaming towards gender equality in the workplace. It is important to take note of the requisite skills needed, as stated in the National Policy Framework for Women's Empowerment and Gender Equality.

Skills required for the actualisation of Gender Equality

(Adapted from National Policy Framework for Women's Empowerment and Gender Equality)[131]

Table 6.2: Thematic skills for implementing gender mainstreaming

Programme Areas	Skills	Outputs
Policy	★ Gender-based analysis; ★ Policy formulation; ★ Programme design; ★ Programme planning.	Gender-sensitive programmes; Plans of action for specific sections of the insitution.
Gender Mainstreaming	★ Statistical analysis; ★ Gender-based analysis; ★ Training skills; ★ Research skills; ★ Planning.	Disaggregated data integration of gender into daily activities; Clear planning programmes.
Co-ordination and Planning	★ Strategic planning; ★ Communication skills; ★ Quantitative and qualitative evaluation skills; ★ Co-ordination.	Management information system; Consensus about the implementation of gender programmes at the organisation.
Advocacy	★ Social and Economic skills; ★ Research/analytical skills; ★ Planning; ★ Training; ★ Monitoring and evaluation.	Common understanding of gender equality and its role in transformation.
Liaison Networking	★ Communication; ★ Grasp of stakeholders' interests; ★ Organisational skills; ★ Report writing.	Clear communications across units at the organisation and external to the organisation.
Capacity Building	★ Management skills; ★ Training; ★ Facilitation skills; ★ Analytical skills; ★ Insight into social situation.	Training manuals; Skilled staff; Best practices/ worst practices and documentation thereof .

As a Human Resource practitioner, it is imperative to concretise gender mainstreaming in formal policies at your organisation. With the advent of the #MeToo campaign it has become increasingly evident that issues of gender sensitivity and awareness need to be mainstreamed through policy. It is therefore important to create a workspace that supports the goal of gender equality through the development and implementation of key policy. Given that we live in a time that is digitised and the move towards a paperless environment, it is in your interest to develop and provide an online policy and procedures system to allow for, amongst other elements, ease of reference.

Often a volume of information is provided to employees at their induction. Policies are usually shared at this stage and then put away for referral. Employees do not know which policies are important or how to implement them. An up-to-date, online system will permit those who use or are directly affected by policies and procedures to have the access they need. This also reduces the cost of printing several policies as information packs when employees are appointed. An online system is further favourable as this allows for them to be readily available. An employee is therefore not reliant on another member to avail the policy as a resource.

Online policies can be easily updated with the newest version being sent via a link to a central system with little cost to the organisation. This allows the employer to adapt to new laws or changes in the economy. Policies must be accompanied by procedures to ensure that those who access the broad policies are guided in the "how to" aspect.

In writing policies and procedures, the following should be considered and has been adapted from the University of California[132]:

★ Policies are written in clear, concise, simple language.

★ Policy statements address what is the rule rather than how to implement the rule.

★ Policy statements are readily available to employees and their authority is clear.

★ Designated "policy experts" (identified in each document) are readily available to interpret policies and resolve problems.

Further considerations for policy development include the use of concise language, the use of facts, the non-use of information that can be outdated, for example, personal information of employees, the use of acronyms must be clearly spelt out and instructions (if any) must be included. The function of a policy is to ensure understanding by employees at all levels. This loosely translates into making policies as easily understood by the lay person. The emphasis is not in fact on high-level or over-complicated English; rather, the focus must be on *understanding* and *application*.

Policies are not simply developed to be shelved (either online or otherwise). Policy owners must make a concerted effort to ensure that policies are understood and that these are implemented as and when an issue arises. Here, the role of a Gender Management Committee must be instrumental in ensuring that policies and procedures are mainstreamed for gender equality. Policy and procedure "owners" are responsible for the timely dissemination, review and update of policies and procedures in their specialised area.

Assignment of responsibility for policies or procedures is usually ascribed at the Executive Committee level. However, this must be delegated to operational staff and must become operational through implementation and strict adherence.

Notable for inclusion in this book is the development of a Sexual Harassment policy. As mentioned earlier, the #MeToo campaign has become almost a global movement for the eradication of gender discrimination and the prevention of sexual harassment. Sexual harassment is unwanted conduct of a sexual nature. The unwanted nature of sexual harassment distinguishes it from behaviour that is welcome and mutual. Sexual attention becomes sexual harassment if:

(a) The behaviour is persisted in, although a single incident of harassment can constitute sexual harassment; and/or

(b) The recipient has made it clear that the behaviour is considered offensive; and/or

(c) The perpetrator should have known that the behaviour is regarded as unacceptable.[133]

The South African Labour Guide is clear on the expectations of employers in providing a workplace free from sexual harassment. Employers are compelled to create and maintain a working environment in which the dignity of employees is respected. In addressing the development of such a policy, it is important to understand the forms of sexual harassment that must be covered.

According to the South African Labour Guide, the forms of sexual harassment are not just limited to physical contact.

1. Sexual harassment may include unwelcome physical, verbal or non-verbal conduct, but is limited to the examples listed as follows:

    a. Physical conduct of a sexual nature includes all unwanted physical contact, ranging from touching to sexual assault and rape, and includes a strip search by or in the presence of the opposite sex.

    b. Verbal forms of sexual harassment include unwelcome innuendoes, suggestions and hints, sexual advances, comments with sexual overtones, sex-related jokes or insults or unwelcome graphic comments about a person's body made in their presence or directed toward them, unwelcome and inappropriate enquiries about a person's sex life, and unwelcome whistling directed at a person or group of persons.

    c. Non-verbal forms of sexual harassment include unwelcome gestures, indecent exposure, and the unwelcome display of sexually explicit pictures and objects.

    d. Quid pro quo harassment occurs where an owner, employer, supervisor, member of management or co-employee, undertakes or attempts to influence the process of employment, promotion, training, discipline, dismissal, salary increment or other benefit of an employee or job applicant, in exchange for sexual favours.

2. Sexual favouritism exists where a person who is in a position of authority rewards only those who respond to his/her sexual advances, whilst other deserving employees who do not submit themselves to any sexual advances are denied promotions, merit rating or salary increases.

The South African Labour Guide is abundantly clear on the principles guiding the implementation of policies around sexual harassment with an emphasis on the responsibility for such a workplace to be the responsibility of all individuals within an organisation. "All employers/management and employees have a role to play in contributing towards creating and maintaining a working environment in which sexual harassment is unacceptable. They should ensure that their standards of conduct do not cause offence and they should discourage unacceptable behaviour on the part of others. Employers/management should attempt to ensure that persons such as customers, suppliers, job applicants and others who have dealings with the business, are not subjected to sexual harassment by the employer or its employees."[134]

Policy statements are a definitive step towards ensuring a commitment, at least on paper, by an organisation in the creation of a workplace free from sexual harassment. Some guiding inputs to policy statements:

    a.   All employees, job applicants and other persons who have dealings with the business, have the right to be treated with dignity.

    b.   Sexual harassment in the workplace will not be permitted or condoned.

    c.   Persons who have been subjected to sexual harassment in the workplace have a right to raise a grievance about it should it occur and appropriate action will be taken by the employer.

3.   Management should be placed under a positive duty to implement the policy and take disciplinary action against employees who do not comply with the policy.

4.   A policy on sexual harassment should also explain the procedure which should be followed by employees who are victims of sexual harassment. The policy should also state that:

    a.   Allegations of sexual harassment will be dealt with seriously, expeditiously, sensitively and confidentially.

    b.   Employees will be protected against victimisation, retaliation for lodging grievances and from false accusations.

5.   Policy statements on sexual harassment should be communicated effectively to all employees.

Policy statements cannot exist in isolation and must be accompanied by procedures for sexual harassment. The latter being a topic of sensitivity, management must ensure that procedures do not allow the victims to be further victimised. Employers and employees must ensure that grievances about sexual harassment are investigated and handled in a manner that ensures that the identities of the persons involved are kept confidential.

In cases of sexual harassment, management, employees and the parties concerned must endeavour to ensure confidentiality in the disciplinary enquiry. Only appropriate members of management as well as the aggrieved person, representative, alleged perpetrator, witnesses and interpreter, if required, must be present at the disciplinary enquiry. Where an employee's existing sick leave entitlement has been exhausted, the employer should give due consideration to the granting of additional sick leave in cases of serious sexual harassment where the employee on medical advice requires trauma counselling.

The Department of Labour stipulates the provision of procedures to address sexual harassment in the workplace. Two procedures are proposed, formal and informal. Where a formal procedure has been chosen by the aggrieved, a formal procedure for resolving the grievance should be available and should:

★   Specify to whom the employee should lodge the grievance.

★   Make reference to timeframes which allow the grievance to be dealt with expeditiously.

★   Provide that if the case is not resolved satisfactorily, the issue can be dealt with in terms of the dispute procedures contained in item 7(7) of the Labour Code of Good Practice.

In an informal procedure, it may be sufficient for the employee concerned to have an opportunity where she/he can explain to the person engaging in the unwanted conduct that the behaviour in question is not welcome, that it offends them or makes them uncomfortable, and that it interferes with their work. If the informal approach has not provided a satisfactory outcome, if the case is severe or if the conduct continues, it may be more appropriate to embark upon a formal procedure. Severe cases may include: sexual assault, rape, a strip search and quid pro quo harassment.

Investigations and formal disciplinary action must be pursued to ensure that sexual harassment is not tolerated in the workplace. Care should be taken during any investigation of a grievance of sexual harassment that the aggrieved person is not disadvantaged, and that the position of other parties is not prejudiced if the grievance is found to be unwarranted. The Code of Good Practice regulating dismissal contained in Schedule 8 of this Act, reinforces the provisions of Chapter VIII of the Labour Act and provides that an employee may be dismissed for serious misconduct or repeated offences. Serious incidents of sexual harassment or continued harassment after warnings are dismissable offences. In cases of persistent harassment or single incidents of serious misconduct, employers ought to follow the procedures set out in the Code of Good Practice contained in Schedule 8 of this Act. The range of disciplinary sanctions to which employees will be liable should be clearly stated, and it should also be made clear that it will be a disciplinary offence to victimise or retaliate against an employee who in good faith lodges a grievance of sexual harassment. Regarding criminal and civil charges, a victim of sexual assault has the right to press separate criminal and/or civil charges against an alleged perpetrator, and the legal rights of the victim are in no way limited by the labour code.

An example of a Sexual Harassment policy is provided below from the South African Kendo Federation[135] The SAKF is the representative body for Kendo, Iaido, and Jodo in South Africa and is affiliated to Martial Arts South Africa (MASA), the International Kendo Federation (FIK) and the European Kendo Federation (EKF). Furthermore, the SAKF is a non-political, non-profit-friendly organisation for its related martial arts regardless of race, colour, religion, sex, age, creed or belief:

A. POLICY STATEMENT

1. The South African Kendo Federation (herein called SAKF) is committed to providing an environment in which all individuals are treated with respect and dignity. Each individual has the right to participate in this environment which promotes equal opportunities and prohibits discriminatory practices. The definition of harassment for the purpose of this policy:

   ★ Harassment is a form of discrimination and/or abuse.

   ★ Harassment is offensive, degrading, and threatening. In its most extreme forms, harassment can be an offence under South African legislation.

   ★ No matter whom the perpetrator, harassment is an attempt by one person to assert abusive, unwarranted power over another.

   ★ The SAKF is committed to providing an environment free of harassment on the basis of race, national or ethnic origin, colour, religion, age, sex, sexual orientation, marital status, family status, or disability.

2. This policy applies to every member of SAKF regardless of their status. The SAKF encourages the reporting of all incidents of harassment, regardless of who the offender may be.

3. This policy applies to harassment which may occur during the course of all SAKF activities and events. It also applies to harassment between individuals associated with SAKF but outside SAKF activities and events when such harassment adversely affects relationships within the SAKF's work and sport environment.

B. DEFINITIONS

4. Harassment is any behaviour by a person or organisation to whom this Policy applies which is offensive, abusive, belittling or threatening and which is directed at a person or a group of people because of a particular characteristic of that person or group of people. The behaviour must be unwelcome and the sort of behaviour a reasonable person would recognise as being unwelcome and likely to cause the recipient to feel offended, humiliated or intimidated. Whether or not the behaviour is Harassment is determined from the point of view of the person receiving the Harassment.

5. Harassment includes:

   a. Sexual Harassment (clauses 6 to 10);

   b. Racial Harassment (clauses 11 and 12);

   c. Sexuality Harassment (clauses 13 to 15);

d.   Disability Harassment (clauses 16 and 17);

e.   Abuse (clauses 18 to 20);

f.   Vilification (clauses 21 to 22);

g.   Discrimination (clauses 23 to 28); and

h.   Victimisation (clause 29).

6.   Sexual Harassment includes:

a.   An unwelcome sexual advance; or

b.   An unwelcome request for sexual favours; or

c)   Any unwelcome conduct of a sexual nature (including a statement, orally or in writing, of a sexual nature), where the person being harassed felt offended, humiliated or intimidated and this was reasonable in the circumstances.

7.   Sexual Harassment is often, but need not be, behaviour which either: (a) involves blackmail, in that the harassment is accompanied by a direct or implied threat, promise or benefit. For example, a coach who implies that a player's selection to a team is dependent on compliance with a sexual proposition; or (b) creates a hostile or sexually permeated environment, in that the harassment consists of crude remarks, jokes, the display of offensive material or makes the environment uncomfortable.

8.   Examples of Sexual Harassment may include:

★   Uninvited touching, kissing, embracing, massaging;

★   Staring, leering, ogling;

★   Smutty jokes and comments;

★   Persistent or intrusive questions about people's private lives;

★   Repeated invitations to go out, especially after prior refusal;

★   The use of promises or threats to coerce someone into sexual activity;

★   The display of sexually explicit material, eg Internet use, computer screen savers, calendars, posters;

★   Getting undressed in front of others of the opposite sex;

★   Invading the privacy of others while showering or toileting;

★   Photographing others while undressing, showering or toileting.

9. Sexual Harassment may be a criminal offence, for example: indecent assault, rape, obscene telephone calls or letters.

10. Sexual behaviour of any kind between an adult and a minor must be reported to the appropriate authorities.

11. Racial Harassment includes harassment based on colour, descent, national or ethnic origin, cultural activity and sometimes religion.

12. Examples of Racial Harassment include:

    ★ Jokes in which race is a significant characteristic of the 'butt' of the joke;

    ★ Hostile comments about food eaten, dress or religious or cultural practices;

    ★ Inferences that all members of a racial or cultural group have particular negative characteristics, such as laziness, drunkenness, greed or sexual promiscuity;

    ★ Parodying accents.

13. Sexuality Harassment includes harassment based on actual or assumed homosexuality, heterosexuality, bi-sexuality or trans-sexuality.

14. Examples of Sexuality Harassment include:

    ★ Jokes in which sexuality is a significant characteristic of the 'butt' of the joke;

    ★ Hostile comments about assumed sexual practices or social activities.

15. In severe cases, such as threats or acts of violence against a homosexual person, Sexuality Harassment may be a criminal offence.

16. Disability Harassment includes harassment based on physical, mental or psychological disability or harassment of an associate or aide of a person with a disability.

17. Examples of Disability Harassment include:

    ★ Jokes where a particular disability is a significant characteristic of the 'butt' of the joke;

    ★ Interfering with a disability aid (eg hearing aid);

    ★ Obstructing a person in a manner that compounds his or her disability (eg putting obstacles in the path of a person with a vision impairment);

    ★ Mocking a person's disability;

    ★ Hostility based on assumed AIDS or HIV infection.

18. Abuse may be a form of Harassment. It includes:

    a. Physical abuse (eg assault);

    b. Emotional abuse (eg blackmail, repeated requests or demands, excluding someone or 'bastardisation' practices);

    c. Neglect (eg failure to provide the basic physical and emotional necessities of life);

    d. Abuse of power, which the harasser holds over the harassed (eg relationships that involve a power disparity include an instructor–student, employer–employee, doctor–patient. People in such positions of power need to be particularly wary not to exploit that power).

19. Examples of abusive behaviour include:

★ Bullying and humiliation of players by instructors;

★ Verbal abuse and insults directed by players or parents at opposing participants;

★ Verbal and/or physical abuse of umpires by players and instructors.

20. Some forms of abuse may constitute a criminal offence, for example, assault and child abuse.

21. Racial Vilification involves a person inciting hatred towards, serious contempt for, or severe ridicule of, a person or group of persons by public act. Public acts that may amount to vilification include any form of communication to the public and any conduct observable by the public.

22. Racial or other forms of Vilification are breaches of this Policy where they are based on any of the attributes or characteristics set out in clause 24.

23. Discrimination is treating or proposing to treat a person less favourably than someone else in certain areas of public life on the basis of an attribute or personal characteristic they have.

24. The applicable attributes or characteristics are:

★ Age;	★ Pregnancy;
★ Disability;	★ Race;
★ Marital status;	★ Religious belief/activity;
★ Parental/Carer status;	★ Sex or gender;
★ Physical features;	★ Sexual orientation;
★ Political belief/activity;	★ Transgender orientation.

25. Not only is Discrimination unlawful, but the organisation and its Affiliated Clubs also consider it is unjust because it may deny people a chance by judging them on the basis of stereotypes or assumptions about what they can or cannot achieve.

26. Discrimination includes direct Discrimination and indirect Discrimination. Direct Discrimination occurs if a person treats, or proposes to treat, someone with an attribute or characteristic less favourably than the person treats or would treat someone without that attribute or characteristic, in the same or similar circumstances. Indirect Discrimination occurs where a person imposes or intends to impose a requirement, condition or practice which on its face is not discriminatory, but has the effect of discriminating against a person(s) with a particular attribute.

27. Requesting, assisting, instructing, inducing or encouraging another person to engage in Discrimination, is also Discrimination.

28. Any behaviour or conduct that is Discrimination under any South African legislation is also Discrimination for the purposes of this Policy.

29. Victimisation occurs where a person is subject to, or is threatened to suffer, any detriment or unfair treatment, because that person has or intends to pursue their legal rights under anti-harassment or anti-discrimination legislation or under this Policy.

C. RESPONSIBILITY

30. The SAKF Executive Committee (EXCO), any other SAKF sub-committee, all affiliated dojo leaders, and instructors of various levels, are responsible for the implementation of this policy. In addition, the SAKF EXCO and all dojo leaders are responsible for:

   ★ Discouraging and preventing harassment within SAKF;

   ★ Investigating formal complaints of harassment in a sensitive, responsible, and timely manner;

   ★ Imposing appropriate disciplinary or corrective measures when a complaint of harassment has been substantiated, regardless of the position or authority of the offender;

   ★ Providing advice to persons who experience harassment;

   ★ Doing all in their power to support and assist any member of SAKF who experiences harassment by someone;

   ★ Making all members of SAKF aware of the problem of harassment, and in particular, sexual harassment, and of the procedures contained in this policy;

★ Informing both complainants and respondents of the procedures contained in this policy of their rights under the law;

★ Regularly reviewing the terms of this policy to ensure that they adequately meet the organisation's legal obligations and public policy objectives;

★ Appointing member protection officers under this policy; and

★ Appointing unbiased case review panels and appeal bodies under this policy.

31. Every member of SAKF has a responsibility to play a part in ensuring that the SAKF environment is free from harassment. This means not engaging in, allowing, condoning, or ignoring behaviour contrary to this policy. In addition, any member of SAKF who believes that a fellow member has experienced or is experiencing harassment is encouraged to notify a member protection officer appointed under this policy.

D.   DISCIPLINARY ACTION

32. Members of SAKF against whom a complaint of harassment is substantiated may be severely disciplined, up to and including the termination of membership in cases where the harassment takes the form of assault, sexual assault, or a related sexual offence.

E.   CONFIDENTIALITY

33. The SAKF understands that it can be extremely difficult to come forward with a complaint of harassment and that it can be devastating to be wrongly convicted of harassment. The SAKF recognises the interests of both the complainant and the respondent in keeping the matter confidential.

34. The SAKF shall not disclose to outside parties the name of the complainant, the circumstances giving rise to a complaint, or the name of the respondent unless such disclosure is required by a disciplinary or the remedial process.

F.   OFFICERS

35. SAKF shall appoint at least two persons, one male and one female, who are themselves members of the organisation, to serve as member protection officers under this policy. If more than two officers are appointed, SAKF shall ensure a gender balance.

36. The role of member protection officers is to serve in a neutral, unbiased capacity and to receive complaints, assist in informal resolution of complaints and investigate formal written complaints. In carrying out their duties under this policy, member protection officers shall be directly responsible to the SAKF [the SAKF President who is responsible for this policy].

G. CODES OF BEHAVIOUR

37. To protect the health, safety and well-being of all the people participating in the activities of the SAKF a set of Codes of Behaviour have been developed and issued. The Codes of Behaviour are set out in Attachment A and form part of this Policy and covers:

★ General Code of Behaviour

★ Administrator Code of Behaviour

★ Students Code of Behaviour

★ Parent/Guardian Code of Behaviour

★ Instructor Code of Behaviour

H. BREACH OF THIS POLICY

38. It is a breach of this Policy for any person or organisation to which this Policy applies to:

a. Fail to comply with any of the responsibilities set out in clauses 30 & 31;

b. Breach any part of the Codes of Behaviour;

c. Engage in any form of Harassment;

d. Make frivolous, vexatious reports of Harassment.

I. GRIEVANCE PROCEDURE

39. A person who experiences harassment is encouraged to make it known to the harasser that the behaviour is unwelcome, offensive, and contrary to this policy.

40. If confronting the harasser is not possible, or if after confronting the harasser the harassment continues, the complainant should seek the advice of a member protection officer.

41. Any person or organisation may make a complaint about a person or group of people to whom this Policy applies, if they consider that person or group of people has, or may have, committed a breach of any part of this Policy.

42. The complaint always belongs to the complainant, who will determine how their complaint is dealt with. The complaint will not be divulged to another person without the complainant's agreement, except those involved in the remedial process or in the case where a person is required by law to report the matter to governmental authorities (for example, in the case of suspected child abuse).

43. It is recommended that complaints are handled, as far as possible, at an informal level. A common-sense, low-key approach is often far more satisfactory to the complainant and to the person complained about.

44. The four principles of case handling will apply at every stage of these procedures. This means that all responsible persons will handle all cases:

   ★ Promptly,

   ★ Seriously,

   ★ Sensitively and

   ★ Confidentially.

45. The member protection officer shall inform the complainant of:

   ★ the options for pursuing an informal resolution of his or her complaint;

   ★ the right to lay a formal written complaint under this policy when an informal resolution is inappropriate or not feasible;

   ★ the confidentiality provisions of this policy;

   ★ the right to be represented by a person of choice (including legal counsel) at any stage in the complaint process; and

   ★ the right to withdraw from any further action in connection with the complaint at any stage (even though SAKF might continue to investigate the complaint).

46. There are four possible outcomes to this initial meeting of complainant and member protection officer:

   a. The complainant and member protection officer agree that the conduct does not constitute harassment.

       i. If this occurs, the member protection officer will take no further action and will make no written record.

   b. The complainant brings evidence of harassment and chooses to pursue an informal resolution of the complaint.

i.   If this occurs, the member protection officer will assist the two parties to negotiate a solution acceptable to the complainant. If desired by the parties and if appropriate, the member protection officer may also seek the assistance of a neutral mediator.

ii.   If informal resolution yields a result which is acceptable to both parties, the member protection officer will make a written record that a complaint was made and was resolved informally to the satisfaction of both parties, and will take no further action.

iii. If informal resolution fails to satisfy the complainant, the complainant will reserve the option of laying a formal written complaint.

c. The complainant brings evidence of harassment and decides to lay a formal written complaint.

i.   If this occurs, the member protection officer will assist the complainant in drafting a formal written complaint, to be signed by the complainant, and a copy given to the respondent without delay. The written complaint should set out the details of the incident(s), the names of any witnesses to the incident(s), and should be dated and signed.

ii.   The respondent will be given an opportunity to provide a written response to the complaint. The member protection officer may assist the respondent in preparing this response.

d. The complainant brings evidence of harassment but does not wish to lay a formal complaint.

i.   If this occurs, the member protection officer must decide if the alleged harassment is serious enough to warrant laying a formal written complaint, even if it is against the wishes of the complainant.

ii.   When the member protection officer decides that the evidence and surrounding circumstances require a formal written complaint, the member protection officer will issue a formal written complaint and, without delay, provide copies of the complaint to both the complainant and the respondent.

47. As soon as possible after receiving the written complaint, but within 21 days, the member protection officer shall submit a report to the SAKF EXCO, containing the documentation filed by both parties along with a recommendation that:

★   No further action be taken because the complaint is unfounded or the conduct cannot reasonably be said to fall within this policy's definition of harassment; or

★　The complaint should be investigated further.

★　A copy of this report shall be provided, without delay, to both the complainant and the respondent.

48. In the event that the member protection officer's recommendation is to proceed with an investigation, the SAKF EXCO, shall within 14 days appoint three (3) appropriate members of the SAKF to serve as a case review panel. This panel shall consist of at least one woman and at least one man. To ensure freedom from bias, no member of the panel shall have a significant personal or professional relationship with either the complainant or the respondent. It should be noted the SAKF EXCO can also appoint themselves as members of the case review panel.

49. Within 21 days of its appointment, the case review panel shall convene a hearing. The hearing shall be governed by such procedures as the panel may decide, provided that:

★　The complainant and respondent shall be given 14 days' notice, in writing, of the day, time and place of the hearing.

★　Members of the panel shall select a chairperson from among themselves.

★　A quorum shall be all three panel members.

★　Decisions shall be by majority vote. If a majority vote decision is not possible, the decision of the chairperson will be the decision of the panel.

★　The hearing shall be held in camera.

★　Both parties shall be present at the hearing to give evidence and to answer questions of the other party and of the panel. If the complainant does not appear, the matter will be dismissed, (unless the complainant decided not to lay a formal complaint, but the officer concluded that the evidence and surrounding circumstances were such as to require a formal written complaint). If the respondent does not appear, the hearing will proceed.

★　The complainant and respondent may be accompanied by a representative or adviser.

★　The member protection officer may attend the hearing at the request of the panel.

50. Within 14 days of the hearing, the case review panel shall present its findings in a report to the SAKF EXCO, which shall contain:

★　a summary of the relevant facts;

★ a determination as to whether the acts complained of constitute harassment as defined in this policy;

★ recommended disciplinary action against the respondent, if the acts constitute harassment; and

★ recommended measures to remedy or mitigate the harm or loss suffered by the complainant, if the acts constitute harassment.

51. If the panel determines that the allegations of harassment are false, vexatious, retaliatory, or unfounded, their report shall recommend disciplinary action against the complainant.

52. A copy of the report of the case review panel shall be provided, without delay, to both the complainant and the respondent.

53. When determining appropriate disciplinary action and corrective measures, the case review panel shall consider factors such as:

★ the nature of the harassment;

★ whether the harassment involved any physical contact;

★ whether the harassment was an isolated incident or part of an ongoing pattern;

★ the nature of the relationship between complainant and harasser;

★ the age of the complainant;

★ whether the harasser had been involved in previous harassment incidents;

★ whether the harasser admitted responsibility and expressed a willingness to change; and

★ whether the harasser retaliated against the complainant.

54. In recommending disciplinary sanctions, the panel may consider the following options, singly or in combination, depending on the severity of the harassment:

★ a verbal apology;

★ a written apology;

★ a letter of reprimand from the sport organisation;

★ referral to counselling;

★ removal of certain privileges of membership;

★ demotion;

★ temporary suspension with or without pay;

★ termination of employment or contract; or

★ expulsion from membership.

55. Where the investigation does not result in a finding of harassment, a copy of the report of the case review panel shall be placed in the member protection officer's files. These files shall be kept confidential and access to them shall be restricted to the SAKF EXCO.

56. Where the investigation results in a finding of harassment, a copy of the report of the case review panel shall be placed in the file of the SAKF EXCO. Unless the findings of the panel are overturned upon appeal, this report shall be retained for a period of ten years, unless new circumstances dictate that the report should be kept for a longer period of time.

J. PROCEDURE WHERE A PERSON BELIEVES THAT A COLLEAGUE HAS BEEN HARASSED

57. Where a person believes that a colleague has experienced or is experiencing harassment and reports this belief to a member protection officer, the officer shall meet with the person who is said to have experienced harassment and shall then proceed in accordance with Section 42.

K. APPEALS

58. Both the complainant and respondent shall have the right to appeal the decision and recommendations of the case review panel. A notice of intention to appeal, along with grounds for the appeal, must be provided to the chairperson of the case review panel within 14 days of the complainant or respondent receiving the panel's report.

59. Permissible grounds for an appeal are:

★ the panel did not follow the procedures laid out in this policy;

★ members of the panel were influenced by bias; or

★ the panel reached a decision which was grossly unfair or unreasonable.

60. In the event that a notice of appeal is filed, the SAKF EXCO shall appoint a minimum of three members to constitute the appeal body. This appeal body shall consist of at least one woman and at least one man. These individuals must have no significant personal or professional involvement with either the complainant or respondent, and no prior involvement in the dispute between them. It should be noted the SAKF EXCO can also appoint themselves as members of the case review panel.

61. The appeal body shall base its decision solely on a review of the documentation surrounding the complaint, including the complainant's and respondent's statements, the reports of the member protection officer and the case review panel, and the notice of appeal.

62. Within ten days of its appointment, the appeal body shall present its findings in a report to the SAKF EXCO. The appeal body shall have the authority to uphold the decision of the panel, to reverse the decision of the panel, and/ or to modify any of the panel's recommendations for disciplinary action or remedial measures.

63. A copy of the appeal body's report shall be provided, without delay, to the complainant and respondent.

64. The decision of the appeal body shall be final.

L. REVIEW AND APPROVAL

65. This policy was approved by the SAKF EXCO on 11 November 2016.

This chapter provided an overview of policy development with a specific focus on the need for engendered workplace policies. An exemplar has been provided for the development of a Sexual Harassment policy. You are advised to ensure that policies such as those influencing supply-chain management and procurement are also mainstreamed for gender equality in line with the relevant regulations that govern preferential procurement. Policies around flexible working hours for overburdened women must also be considered and, contrary to popular belief, will in fact increase productivity. Policy implementation is everyone's responsibility and therefore forms an integral part of the gender mainstreaming strategy at your organisation. The value of the gender action plan therefore cannot be emphasised enough as this plan ensures that mainstreaming happens at all levels.

CHAPTER 7

Holding up a Mirror

Monitoring and evaluation has largely been gender-blind. Very few organisations have successfully managed the implementation of a monitoring and evaluation system that takes gender considerations into account. "Monitoring" and "evaluation" are often used interchangeably; however, it is important to note the differences. Monitoring is the regular collection, analysis and distribution of information and data on the progress of the activities and programmes implemented.[136] Evaluation and impact assessment work at a deeper level. They are two slightly different processes although they both make an assessment of the project or programme against its targets. Evaluation establishes whether the positive outcomes planned by the project have been achieved[137]; impact assessment looks at the positive and negative impact of the project.[138]

Monitoring and evaluation is an important part of a comprehensive gender mainstreaming strategy. To measure the implementation of gender initiatives, such measuring and assessment mechanisms must be gender-sensitive. Depending on project goals, this could mean that they are designed or formulated in such a way as to identify differences between women and men in perceptions, attitudes, opportunities, and access to resources and decision-making. It is also important to assess how such projects, programmes and policies impact on social understandings of what it means to be a woman or a man, on gender relations in the organisation.

The National Policy Framework for Women's Empowerment and Gender Equality provides assistance in this regard. Monitoring and evaluation will serve many functions, but mainly this aspect will assist in ensuring that employers and employees are held accountable for their commitment to gender mainstreaming as a strategy for gender equality. In addition, monitoring and evaluation will assist you in measuring the success and impact of the programmes that seek to implement gender equality principles and will help to measure the effectiveness and impact of policy and in assessing whether, in the long term, there has been a positive impact for women in particular and for the whole society in general. In Chapter 7, I highlight the importance of ongoing documentation through the development of organisational-specific case studies.

Table 7.1: Short-term indicators[139]

Focus area	Indicator
Capacity Building	★ the number and quality of gender training programmes introduced to develop staff gender programming capacity and the number and categories of people trained; ★ the number and quality of in-house programmes (including affirmative action programmes) introduced to enhance women's participation in decision-making structures and the number of women benefiting from such programmes.
Gender Sensitive Staff Recruitment and Discipline	★ the existence of appropriate guidelines for recruitment committees indicating the desired gender mix; ★ the existence of appropriate guidelines for gender awareness training for all staff responsible for recruitment and selection as well as for newly recruited staff; ★ the number and effectiveness of national, provincial and local-level organisations which have developed and utilised gender-sensitive policies and guidelines for reporting and disciplining cases of sexual harassment; ★ the number and effectiveness of internal structures established to deal with gender-based discrimination and sexual harassment.

Gender Sensitive Terms and Conditions of Service which address Practical Gender Needs	★ The extent to which gender-sensitive and responsive programmes have been established to enhance the roles of both male and female employees as parents and professionals, e.g. day-care centres in the work place.
Women's Increased Access to Management and Leadership	★ Increased levels of skills in gender sensitivity and analysis among all managers; ★ Increased number of women at senior management level, aiming for a 50/50 ratio.
Transformation in the Allocation of Resources	★ the level of human and financial resources allocated to programmes to advance women's empowerment and gender equality; ★ equal employment opportunity expenditure by organisations on their employees (for example, the training for women managers, and job descriptions which reflect equal employment opportunities); ★ gender mainstreaming of budget allocations and expenditures.
Data Collection and Utilisation	★ effective process of production and utilisation of gender-disaggregated data and statistics; ★ gender-disaggregated data collection that reflects the relevant situation, problems and concerns of women and men; ★ gender-disaggregated data and statistics reviewed and updated regularly for use in programme development, planning and implementation; ★ adequate capacity (human and financial) for the collection, analysis and dissemination of gender-related statistics.

Whilst the table above provides examples of indicators, it is important to understand what the terms in the table mean. Gender-disaggregated data is essentially data related to the inclusion/exclusion of men and women in project data. Gender is however one aspect of disaggregation which often includes age, geographic location, ethnic group, disability, etc. Disaggregated data cannot show hidden elements such as the influence of power or social standing. These factors play an important role in understanding the disaggregated data.

> ## 💼 Case:
>
> *In an impact assessment study conducted by Action Aid in Bangladesh, preferences for change expressed by men and women varied. While they were both in agreement about the hope for increased income, men gave higher priority to changes related to women's development than the women themselves. On the other hand, though, women gave higher priority to access to loans, increased decision-making and greater mobility for women.[140]*

This case demonstrates the differently expressed needs and preferences of women and men but does not show the power relations that influence these preferences. Indicators must be both qualitative and quantitative and must include contextual factors. Indicators must measure empowerment by looking at the changes (if any) in the attitudes of men and women in the workplace. Disaggregated data, as mentioned earlier, must be accompanied by more in-depth research to look at the factors influencing why data is reflected in the manner in which it is.

As a Human Resource practitioner, it is difficult to ultimately hold all role players accountable for their participation in or absentia from gender mainstreaming initiatives. There are however some mechanisms that you can consider:

★   Ensure that your organisation captures disaggregated statistics.

★   Mainstream your performance indicators.

★   Properly estimate targets.

★   Introduce gender auditing systems and possibly systems of gender budgeting.

It is important to consider some barriers to the implementation of your monitoring and evaluation initiatives. This is closely linked to the Gender Action Plan mentioned earlier and must be addressed in the development thereof. These barriers include:

★   Low level of gender awareness among the staff of the programme at the policy-making and/or implementation levels. This results in incorrect assumptions on women's roles and needs which are not based on factual information, make women's work invisible and neglect women's potential to participate in and benefit from your initiatives.

★ Lack of gender specificity in the programme document.

★ Insufficient representation of women and women's organisations in the programme's steering or advisory committee(s).

★ Low level of gender awareness among the target of initiatives.

★ Existence of socio-cultural norms that lack gender awareness and sensitivity.

★ Low commitment or interest among women because the programme does not address their needs or increases their workload.

★ Lower educational levels of women.

★ Organisational arrangements such as the timing, location or duration of project activities which may form a barrier to women's participation.

★ Use of communication channels which are not accessible to women and men.

The most important lessons the Catholic Agency for Overseas Development (CAFOD), Oxfam and the Agency for Cooperation and Research in Development (ACORD) learnt from their reviewing processes are:

★ The need to listen and learn from staff and Southern counterparts, because gender relations differ from one culture to another and are an integral part of that culture.

★ The inadequacy of some of the tools and models developed in the North by academics and NGOs, and the need constantly to question and re-think the issues and approaches.

★ The time required to work on an issue which affects staff and counterparts at both a personal and a professional level: a long-term perspective is essential when trying to address real issues of social change.

★ The need for real staff commitment and money to work on the issue, accepting that there will be no quick results.[141]

You are encouraged to look at the issue of collaborations as outlined in previous chapters. These collaborations can and will assist you to develop an implementation strategy that includes a well-balanced gender-sensitive monitoring and evaluation strategy. These implementation strategies can go a long way in providing longevity for your projects and programmes and will ultimately shift your policies from being paper exercises to *real* experiences.

As mentioned earlier, the Commission for Gender Equality is a Chapter nine institution tasked with mainstreaming gender in the country. Part of their function is to strengthen constitutional democracy. This body releases various research pieces from their research unit on an annual basis which is in the public domain. You are encouraged to seek out the latest research and ground-breaking cases from the Commission for Gender Equality to inform the gender mainstreaming work in your organisation.

Gender-sensitive criteria is the main trigger point for the successful implementation of a gender action plan and the success of the overall strategy is largely dependent on this element. Below is an example of gender-sensitive evaluation criteria[142]:

Relevance: Has the project/programme effectively contributed to the creation of favourable conditions for gender equality? Did it respond to the practical and strategic gender needs of women? Was the treatment of gender equality issues throughout the implementation phase logical and coherent? Were adjustments made to respond to external factors of the project/programme (e.g. economic crisis, new government etc.) which influenced gender relationships?

Efficiency: Has the implementation of the policy been efficient with respect to gender equality? Are the means and resources being used efficiently to achieve results in terms of improved benefits for both women and men? Have the results for women and men been achieved at reasonable cost, and have costs and benefits been allocated and received equitably?

Effectiveness: Did the project/programme results turn out to be effective in achieving gender equality? Have the results contributed to the achievement of the planned results and outcomes, and have benefits favoured male and/or female target groups? Did stakeholders (organisations, institutions, indirect target groups) benefit from the interventions in terms of institutional capacity-building in the area of gender mainstreaming and the development of gender competence among their staff?

Impact: What has been the impact of the project's outcomes on wider policies, processes and programmes which enhance gender equality and women's rights? For example, did it contribute to a more balanced distribution of unpaid care labour and family responsibilities between women and men? A gender-specific ex-post evaluation can also be used for projects/programmes without a gender equality perspective and will assess whether these have produced any (positive or negative) unintended or unexpected impacts on gender relations.

Sustainability: Are achievements in gender equality likely to be sustained after funding ends? To what extent has ownership of the policy goals been achieved by male and female beneficiaries? To what extent have strategic gender needs of women and men been addressed through the project, and has this resulted in sustainable improvement of women's rights and gender equality? To what extent has capacity for gender mainstreaming through the project been built and institutionalised?

Senior management must ultimately be held accountable for driving gender mainstreaming initiatives in your organisation. As a Human Resource practitioner your job is to provide the capacitation for employees (at all levels) to implement a change with regard to gender equality. It is therefore important to host an informal evaluation besides the formal measures outlined above.

The South African State has implemented, what has been called "Senior Management Services Roundtables" (SMS Roundtables). The SMS Roundtable should be reviewed as a mechanism for the mainstreaming of gender. These forums are convened bi-annually to engage the issue of gender mainstreaming at senior management level. These forums usually exclude men and notably exclude the interests of women at lower management echelons and thus provide a skewed representation of interests. The forums can be used as a mechanism to check on the implementation of gender mainstreaming in an organisation. This forms an informal type of evaluation and can be applied across sectors. The forums should be run at a senior level to engage with senior management in order to gauge their barriers to implementation but also to engage on the successful mainstreaming initiatives.

In addition, you may consider looking at an impact assessment of your strategies. It is imperative that initiatives are looked at from inception to impact in order to assess their effectiveness. Evaluation and impact assessment work at a deeper level. They are two slightly different processes although they both make an assessment of the project or programme against its targets. Evaluation establishes whether the positive outcomes planned by the project have been achieved[143]; impact assessment looks at the positive and negative impact of the project.[144]

How to approach gender impact assessment?

★ Establish the nature of gender relations in spheres relevant to the project (eg. access and control of resources, control of incomes within the household, patterns of expenditure within the household if these are the gender relations that are more likely to affect the impact of the project).

★ Consider the potential impacts of the project on gender relations (useful to analyse possible outcomes, and adjust the project/programme accordingly).

★ Establish the information required and design appropriate indicators (disaggregate all data, consider the impact on gender relations).

★ Collect and analyse the data using appropriate tools and techniques (quantitative and qualitative).

★ Carry out the process in gender-sensitive ways.[145]

This chapter looked at how to reflect on your organisational performance in the implementation of gender mainstreaming as a transformation strategy aimed at gender equality. These tools can be adapted to your context and must be considered with the support of your stakeholders and senior management.

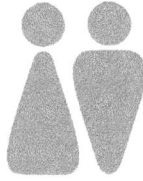

CHAPTER 8

Longevity

The use of case study development is explained in this chapter with reference to how to develop cases to capture lessons. The value of the worst case is discussed for its importance in learning in the workplace. The case studies will form onboard resources for you as a Human Resource practitioner, developed and driven by yourself, as lessons that can be referred to in the longevity of the organisation. These case studies will seek to document the lived experiences of implementing gender mainstreaming strategies and forms part of an ongoing reflective evaluation as to what works and how to address the barriers that inhibit certain initiatives.

Developing a case study is essentially a research-based exercise. This skill may be a bit rusty as many of us last used research methodologies when studying. Johansson[146] claims that the case study is a meta-method, meaning that several research methods are combined. A case may be chosen due to being information-rich, critical or extreme amongst other criteria. This is opposed to how cases are selected for a representational sample.[147] A case is generally selected as there is a vested interest in the findings that may emerge. The case study method is therefore applicable as this provides the required data without having to employ a very labour-intensive research method.

That being said, you as the Human Resource practitioner now have another hat as researcher. You will have to decided on how to collect data that will inform your case study. Discussion on qualitative and quantitative methods is necessary. Qualitative research attempts to unearth information on everyday life for various communities in a natural setting. Denzin and Lincoln[148] explain that, "...qualitative research involves an interpretive, naturalistic approach to its subject matter; it attempts to make sense of, or to interpret, phenomena in terms of the meaning people bring to them." According to Domegan and Fleming,[149] "Qualitative research aims to explore and to discover issues about the problem on hand, because very little is known about the problem. There is usually uncertainty about dimensions and characteristics of the problem. It uses "soft" data and gets "rich" data.

Myers[150] argues that qualitative research assists with unearthing how people and social contexts operate. Qualitative studies allow the complexities of real life to be explored and represented. Qualitative data sources include the researcher's impressions, observation and participant observation (fieldwork), interviews and questionnaires, documents and texts. Data emanate from direct observation of behaviours, interviews, written opinions, or from public documents.[151] Combinations of written descriptions of people, events, opinions, attitudes and environments can also be sources of data.

There are some risks attached to using this method:

Some of the risks are that:

★ The researcher's bias can influence the design of a study.

★ The researcher's bias can enter into data collection at the Department.

★ Sources or subjects may not all be equally credible given that not all share the same values.

★ Some subjects may be previously influenced and affect the overall outcome of the study.

★ Background information may be missing/absent or withheld.

The last point is particularly pertinent as it is therefore your responsibility to document accurately with the information provided and acknowledge in your case study that in fact, some information is missing.

Quantitative research, as discussed by Denzin and Lincoln,[152] presents statistical results and qualitative research presents data as descriptive narration. This is further supported by Hittleman and Simon[153] who claim:

120

Quantitative research makes use of questionnaires, surveys and experiments to gather data that is revised and tabulated in numbers, which allows the data to be characterised by the use of statistical analysis.

Notably, research methodologies will have to suit the organisational make-up and must also be cost-effective. The research component is often outsourced because of the tendencies of case writers to reflect their own biases. A practical step to address this would be for you to share (with permission) your case study report with a peer organisation as a reviewer to check whether the case is written with bias. In the development of case studies, the validity of research is often questioned. There is therefore a need to use triangulation when writing up a case for your organisation.

Validating your case

In order to validate your case you must use a variety of sources to confirm your emerging findings. Often, relying on interviews alone can be detrimental to formulating a case. It is advisable to reflect on the use of reports emanating from your organisation as well as industry trends to assess how well you are doing as an organisation in terms of gender equality. Triangulation validates results of a study to unearth any biases if they do exist. Triangulation incorporates multiple data sources.[154] Richie and Lewis[155] state that: "The security that triangulation provides is through giving a fuller picture of phenomena, not necessarily a more certain one." Duneier[156] believes that one should constantly check and re-check the consistency of the findings, from different as well as the same sources.

Triangulation was developed through the need to confirm the validity of a process in a case study. The verification therefore can be done using a variety of sources.[157] In order to confirm your case, the use of additional materials adds credibility. This approach employs a plethora of data, for example, observation, report checking, etc. Multiple perspectives can verify or refute claims... According to Creswell[158] and Patton,[159] triangulation is used to compare data to decide if it is valid. (See also Blaikie, 2000; Scandura & Williams, 2000). The value of multiple perspectives cannot be stressed enough as this allows for the recipients of case studies to assess other points of view that reiterate and validate your findings.

Ultimately, whatever is gleaned from participants in a study cannot merely be accepted as truth. These testimonies, whether through interviews or surveys, must be verified using documentation. Available reports either from their managers or performance reports will be able to verify claims made. Again, research available in the public domain (not necessarily academic), such as Statistics South Africa reports and reports from the Human Sciences Research Council, will assist in providing the verification of data. In addition, it is important to provide trend reports emanating from the informal evaluation techniques punted in the previous chapter i.e. the roundtable discussions.

Capturing the case

It is important to obtain approval from your Executive before capturing cases. You should choose a theme that is within your reach and doable within the given financial period. Note that a case study must be limited to a certain period and must be stated as such. It is important that any case that is captured is based on projects that have been completed and not on projects that are ongoing. This is to safeguard the case writer as the outcome is already known. The case is therefore written retrospectively. Each case has its own limitations, and this must be stated upfront, for example:

HR Research Case 12:

This case study focuses on the success of capacity interventions at Senior Management level at Blink Solutions in addressing gender budgeting practices. The case addresses whether skills transfer translated into meaningful changes in budget allocations at Blink Solutions for the period 1 January 2017 to 31 December 2017.

This case is therefore narrow in scope and can be addressed through a process of consultation with senior management. The testimonies of participants in the research case can therefore also be verified through an inspection of the budget allocations for the given time period, 1 January 2017 to 31 December 2017. When you write a case study, you must write with the reader in mind. All cases must be written with a learning objective in mind, i.e. what information would you like to capture to form a repository of information for your organisation? Case studies are not designed for large groups or for too wide a sample size. The case study is therefore limited and must provide key information that future Human Resource practitioners and managers can refer to.

You must narrow down your research goal. Here are the main types of case studies, organised by goal:[160]

★ Illustrative case studies describe an unfamiliar situation in order to help people understand it. For instance, a case study of a manager who is making headway in the rollout of projects. What are the key elements that allow this manager to succeed as opposed to other managers within your organisation with the same set of circumstances?

★ Exploratory case studies are preliminary projects to help guide a future, larger-scale project. They aim to identify research questions and possible research approaches. For example, in a case study of three projects, describe the pros and cons of each approach, and give tentative recommendations on how a new project could be organised.

★ Critical instance case studies focus on unique cases, without a generalised purpose. Examples include a descriptive study of a project approaching a rare management dilemma to determine whether a broadly applied "universal" approach is actually applicable or useful in all cases.

When conducting the case study you must ensure that you undertake the necessary background research for the area you are capturing for longevity of learning. Look at how the project came into being and the key reasoning behind it. Unearth the strategies that were used that ultimately led to the success or failure thereof. For example:

> **Recruitment strategy for attracting more women in senior management**
> What target was set? Did the target have a further racial or disability component? Why was the target defined in this manner? What existing barriers were identified that led to the recruitment of more women at senior management level?

Learn how to conduct Obtrusive Observation. This technique allows you to be immersed in the subject of your researcher and you are no longer seen as a "spy". Establishing trust will allow participants in your research to feel more at ease. Having the participants fill out a questionnaire will also provide for a more positive uptake of your case study. When subjects know they are being studied, they are often quick to change their behaviour; the completion of an anonymous questionnaire can therefore offer a "safe" alternative to observation.[161]

It is important to verify your questionnaire with an anonymous interview. Depending on the length of your study, you may want to conduct weekly, monthly or even bi-monthly interviews in capturing your case. You do not simply arrange meetings and conduct interviews on the spot; a certain degree of planning must be undertaken. You must select the type of interview you are going to conduct:

★ Individual face-to-face (choose non-shy participants willing to share).

★ Telephone (not ideal but used when direct access is not possible).

★ Focus group (if time is limited, if interaction aids response, if solo participants are hesitant).

The benefits of undertaking interviews is that the researcher sets the pace of the interview. The historical context can be provided by the interviewee. Note also that there are some drawbacks to be aware of:

★ Researcher's presence may introduce biased responses.

★ Responses are indirect (out of context from actual performance as in field observation) and may be filtered by interviewee.

You then have the important task of formulating questions ahead of the interview. You must ascertain what you would like to gain from the interview. In other words, how does the interview assist you in fulfilling the purpose of your case? In formulating or asking questions:

★ Determine what kind of information is needed before writing questions.

★ Keep questions open-ended, unstructured e.g. " tell a story about ...."; "trace ... back to the beginning" ... "walk me through the process you experienced ...".

★ Ask clear questions.

★ Ask single questions.

★ Use few in number (no more than five).

★ Memorise questions and their order (follow three stages):

   - Stage 1: establish interviewee background in area of research.

   - Stage 2: details of present experience relevant to topic.

   - Stage 3: meaning the current experience has for them.

★ Match level of questions and probes to ability of interviewee.

★ To get information you need to allow for exploration but stay on track regarding themes of questions; assure you are well versed in the terminology and the background on the topic; and use probes, contradict, link, challenge, encourage and acknowledge/show understanding.

★ Be a good listener (offer little advice and few questions; ask for details, clarification, examples, allow for silence while participant thinks).

It is in your interest to provide your participant with an interview protocol form ahead of the actual interview. Unlike job interviews, the research participant could also benefit from being provided with the questions ahead of time in order to gather the necessary information, facts and figures required.

Exemplar

Date:

Time:

Location of interview:

Details of interviewer:

Notes to interviewee:

Thank you for your participation. I believe your input will be valuable to this research and in helping grow all of our professional practice.

Confidentiality of responses is guaranteed.

Approximate length of interview: 30 minutes, five major questions.

Purpose of research: To determine the factors needed for units to achieve 50/50 quotas in the appointment of female employees

i.   What challenges do they face?

ii.   What are the cultural norms for interview practices?

iii.   What are the challenges for the unit as a whole?

iv.   What are the motivations for the appointment of women?

v.   What factors are deemed important when recruiting for the unit?

Methods of disseminating results: This can be determined according to the case method. Sometimes results can be emailed with the relevant stats, while at other times a presentation is perhaps more suited for sensitive subjects.

Building on the theme of recruiting more women as the subject of the case study, below are some generic questions that can be adapted for the purpose of interviewing managers responsible for the recruitment of more women at senior management level.

1. Take me back through the history in your career that brought you to this institute. What types of professional development have you previously experienced at this organisation and others? What is an area of strength or expertise for you? (These questions put the interviewee at ease.)

2. Do you think it is important to recruit more women at senior management level? (Why or why not?). Can you describe some key skills and experience that you think women at senior management should possess? Is this experience similar to that which you expect of men? (This question will reveal the gender biases of the interviewee, should any exist.)

3. Can you walk me through the learning processes availed to you in the recruitment of new staff? Have your feelings about doing recruitment changed during your time at the organisation? (This question establishes the willingness to undertake the recruitment process.)

4. What factors most helped/hindered the recruitment process? Why? How? Here is a list of potential factors that may help you... What were some challenges you faced in the recruitment process? Why? What activities gave you the most success in achieving your goal of recruiting women at senior management level? Why? (This question elicits the level of experience and assistance provided to those with decision-making powers.)

> 5. Can you describe a specific incident that sparked significant growth for women at your institute? If no incident comes to mind, how about a task or exercise? Why was this incident significant? What will the future impact of this incident be on the position of women in senior management? (This question speaks to the need for an enabling environment to nurture talent at senior management level.)

The interview process is an important piece of the case study writing process as the interviews provide you with the data that will be used to inform the outcome of the case. Again, it is important to write cases on projects or processes that have been completed and that are not still ongoing. The exemplar above provides generic questions that can be adapted for a theme. However, there are many questions that inform your case study from the Human Resources perspective[162].

★ Which of your employees will this case study target?

★ What problem did they need solved?

★ Why do you think person or persons X were chosen to help them solve it?

★ How did they approach the challenge?

★ What was the ultimate solution, and how long did it take to implement?

★ What benefits or results from the work could be seen immediately?

★ What benefits or results could be seen over time?

Case studies provide self-guided research. Below are broad headings that can be populated by providing answers to the suggested questions. This information, as well as information gleaned from interviews with key staff, will assist you in the development of a case study that will form a resource for your organisation. You must write the case study for someone who has not interacted with the project being captured, meaning that you must write the case study for someone who has no knowledge of your organisation or the projects/staff/resources that lie within it.

As a point of departure, you must write the background information. In this section you will basically be providing the information that contextualises your organisation and the project you are highlighting therein.

The following questions can be considered:

★ Which of your employees will this case study target?

Limit your answer to one or two persons. If you have a more clearly-defined audience, your message is more likely to resonate with the right people.

★ Does this case study relate to a specific product, service, or vertical? If so, which?

★ What should this case study demonstrate to your readers about your organisation?

Next you must contextualise the project or process being documented. "About the project/process":

★ Express whether permission has been ascertained for the capturing of the case study from your Executive Authority.

★ What is the full name of the specific project or process?

★ What are important details about this project/process that should be shared?

★ Do they have multiple locations? If so, which location will this case study focus on?

★ Do you have any testimonials that can be included in this case study? The testimonials help to validate claims made. (Note that this is separate from the interview process described above and can be solicited anonymously.)

Outline the challenge. This is an important piece of the case study writing as it seeks to provide the problem that was being solved. Even if attempts at solving this problem have failed, this still constitutes institutional knowledge that cannot and should not be lost. What issue, challenge, or pain point did the project address? Why did this problem exist? If the project is part of the core functions of your organisation, state this as such. Or was the project an unforeseen consequence of another action? What were the expected outcomes from the project? This answer is critical, as you will circle back to it when addressing your results.

The project solutions must also be documented methodically to ensure that solutions are part of your institutional knowledge and therefore mistakes/ problems can be remedied easily as the problem/challenge has been addressed before.

Consider the following:

★ How did you approach the challenge?

★ Did you base your response on experience, or was it a brand new challenge that required you to think outside of the box?

★ What research did you conduct?

★ Who on your organisational team was involved?

★ Who did you collaborate with on a strategy?

★ Did you collect feedback to inform what your ultimate solution would look like?

★ Were there pilot or testing phases?

★ What was the ultimate solution?

★ What did the solution look like?

★ What products or platforms were developed/deployed or used?

★ Why did your organisation make those choices? (Remember, only include details here that your target persons would care about.)

★ What was the timeline? (This is very useful in informing how long it will take to solve a similar challenge in the future.)

★ How long did it take to plan/design/develop your solution? How long did it take to implement?

Finally, and perhaps most significantly, you must capture the results whether these are positive or negative. Again, there are notable learning points for both best-case and worst-case scenarios. Each case has value in its own merit. Notably, the factors or elements such as resourcing (both financial and human) must be documented to indicate their influence on project results.

★ Did your solution solve the stated problem or accomplish the objective(s)?

★ What results were immediately evident? (Increased employee productivity? A better system, platform or software solution?)

★ There can also be soft results such as better working relationships, better collaborations etc.)

★ What benefits became evident over time? (Increased sales? Reduced turnover? Improved collaboration?)

★ Are there specific Key Performance Areas, measurements, statistics or Return on Investment data you can share that clearly demonstrate the value of the solution/service/strategy you provided?

Please include what each statistic is, as well as over what period it was measured and its relevance to the client's objective, for example, a 150% increase in the appointment of women at senior management level. Which one of those data points would you consider to be the most important? Why? Finally, would your senior management agree that the project solved the problem or helped them achieve their intended goal? The latter must be carefully considered in consultation with your Executive Authority.

Gender Mainstreaming Case Study Example[163]

Project A was designed to respond to organisational strengthening needs of an association of professionals – let's call it Stars Alliance – and to contribute to improving the quality of the profession. Gender mainstreaming was included in the Project's Work Plan as a cross-cutting theme, yet its practical implication remained to be investigated and followed-up. The Project indicators were not gender-disaggregated at the start of the Project.

During its inception phase, the Project team used the stakeholders' analysis to understand their roles, needs and situation. At the start of the Project, 30% of the Stars Alliance members were women. Yet, there were no women on its board and there were less than 10% of them in other internal management committees. Women have organised themselves into an association, let's call it WLA.

WLA was established in March 2015 by 8 women lawyers. It was a young and small association with high aspirations to promote gender equality both within Stars Alliance and on the legal services market. The WLA was marginalised within the Alliance and its voice was weak. None of its initiatives, including gaining equal treatment of women professionals within social security, were supported by the Alliance.

The Project's Stakeholders Analysis increased the understanding that for the gender mainstreaming to be successful, the WLA voice had to be heard and its capacity had to be strengthened. Moreover, including WLA in the Project meant that it would have the same effects and impact on men and women, both at the level of capacity and skills. A number of gender-sensitive indicators were introduced, for example, the number of women in the Bar pool of trainers; the number of women candidates for management positions and the number of women elected/selected in management committees.

Thus, the Project team pursued a pro-active role in involving WLA in the Project. The Project insisted on including WLA in all consultations organised to prepare the Stars Alliance Management Road Map, draft its Organisational Strategy for 2017–2022 and its Communication Strategy. The Project also consistently included WLA representatives in all Project workshops, conferences and seminars, breaking down little by little the isolation previously experienced. WLA was also included in the Project's Steering Committee enabling the organisation to make contributions and participate in decision making.

In addition to that, the Project implemented a number of activities designed specifically to strengthen WLA capacity as an organisation. As a result of these, WLA prepared its own Strategy for 2018–2023, started to collaborate with a similar organisation at the European level, organised its general assembly on a regular basis, multiplied by ten the number of its members, gained space on the Alliance website (where it can regularly publish its news and make itself visible and heard) and presented an alternative report on the women's rights situation in the country at the UN Committee for Social, Economic and Cultural rights in Geneva.

All of the above contributed to making the WLA voice heard within the Alliance and externally, empowering it to take gender mainstreaming forward to the benefit of the profession.

The Project's approach to increase the capacity of WLA brought two lessons learned:

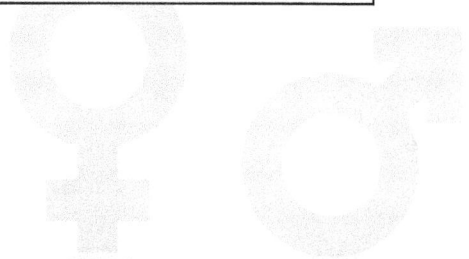

a. the Project had to be ready to mitigate risks of occasional disengagement from the Alliance management in Project activities, when WLA-lead activities were perceived as challenging to the organisational culture that existed since its establishment.

b. helping WLA to form partnerships - e.g. with the European women professional associations - was an important part of the sustainability of the action, as it anchored it in a network of organisations, which share similar challenges and aspirations.

I hope that you will be inspired to implement the case study method in capturing the successes and failures of your organisation. Essentially this forms a repository for yourself and future Human Resource practitioners at your organisation. The data that emerges from the development of case studies provides longevity for projects and allows you, as the Human Resource practitioner, to also practise introspection as to how to go about gender mainstreaming initiatives.

CHAPTER 9

Sustainable Campaigns

In the age of information, it is important for you to understand the value of constant messaging and its relationship to sustainable gender equality campaigns. The notion of campaigns is explored in the physical and digital space. These initiatives are highlighted for their value in driving the goals of the Gender Action Plans that will be developed for the entire organisation. Campaigns are often synonymous with internal marketing. You will have to launch an internal marketing campaign. With an internal marketing strategy, employees are treated as "internal customers" who must be convinced of a company's vision and worth just as aggressively as "external customers".

Campaigns around gender equality are difficult to sustain and develop. You must therefore look at who the target audience is and understand what their barriers to receiving information may be. This will inform your strategy. You will have to decide on whether your campaign could be digital or perhaps a physical messaging campaign in the form of posters and leaflets in the office. The idea is to provide a targeted intervention for all employees to understand what gender equality is and why it is important. Your main aim is to align the goals and attitudes of employees towards gender equality as the ultimate outcome. Your campaign essentially must create an awareness of the importance of the overall goal of gender equality and lead to action. Reflect on the success of the campaign below:

#HeForShe[164]

A solidarity movement initiated by UN Women, the campaign #HeForShe engaged men to advocate the message of gender equality. Kick-starting a global conversation, this campaign aimed at reaching out on a global level to spread the message of equality. Emma Watson became the face of this brand and she is also the goodwill ambassador of UN Women.

Given the nature of gender equality campaigns, you must expect resistance. Campaigns are not about information sharing, and with gender equality, you are looking to change mindsets which have been entrenched quite literally since childhood. You already know your context but if not, and you feel that you want some confirmation, please undertake a gender audit before embarking on the implementation of a gender equality campaign. Knowing your audience is ultimately the key to a successful gender equality campaign. Try mapping out the forces for and against what you want to happen. Draw a map of the problem – the people involved, the organisations – and work out exactly what the mechanisms are for the decisions you want to change.

The KISS principle is applicable for both internal and external campaigns. In this case, you want to communicate a clear message to your internal customers using the 'Keep it Simple Stupid' (KISS) principle. Communicate only one thing at a time so as to get the message out. Use a simple unambiguous 'call to action' which requires no explanation. You need to follow the sequence: > awareness > alignment > engagement > action. Each stage will require careful consideration in order to achieve the overall result of employees motivating themselves to act. The campaign involves a deliberate series of revelations or communication exercises to take your employees from an assumed state of ignorance, through interest and then concern (components of awareness), into engagement (motivation), and finally into a state of satisfaction or reward. Showing a problem may lead to concern but, in itself, that won't lead to action. Show them now is the opportunity to force a change, to implement the solution, and give them a way to act – and you have the conditions for engagement. Reflect on the case below:

Are You Man Enough To Be A Nurse?[165]

This campaign was an attempt to tackle the other side of the gender divide. Nursing is still an overwhelmingly female profession, with many men put off by the idea of it being emasculating or effeminate.

Back in 2002 the Oregon Center for Nursing (OCN) ran a recruitment campaign aimed at tackling this image, with the tagline: "Are You Man Enough to Be a Nurse?"

The idea behind the campaign is clear: it's an attempt to counter the femininity associated with the profession. Despite initial acclaim by the American Association of Male Nurses (AAMN), critics questioned the need to masculinize the career. In a sense, it's just as patronizing as the "feminizing" of STEM careers in an attempt to appeal to women.

The AAMN eventually agreed and in 2009 decided to focus less on masculinity/femininity and instead introduce a new campaign: "Do what you love and you'll love what you do." The new focus is on "de-gentrifying" nursing, emphasizing instead the personal strengths and interests of applicants.

The most successful campaigns are ones which challenge the labels we place on society, rather than reinforcing them. For universities looking to widen the diversity of their applicants, whether that's women in science or men in nursing, the key is to approach the question in a non-patronising manner.

Framing your messages is perhaps the most important part of your campaign. Directly or indirectly, a campaign consists of persuading others not just that you are right but that you are so right that they must take some form of action. The simplest thing you can do to help your message is to be direct and straightforward. Forget about being 'clever'. When all else fails (as it probably will): say what you mean.[166]

Gender equality is very broad in scope and therefore you must narrow the scope of your campaign to reach your audience to address a problem. Choose an issue that will transform the lives of women and girls in your workplace. For example, if your problem is sexual harassment in the workplace, how will you approach this topic with your audience? What action do you want them to take? Decide on the campaign aim using a gender lens. Challenge stereotypes in communications by looking at how you select language and images. Most gender campaigns feature pictures of female models and girls;

perhaps challenge this stereotype by looking at the use of symbols and pictures of men. This frames a new way of thinking and links men as partners in the struggle for change.

Gender Equality versus Women's rights[167]

Some organisations use the concept of gender equality and focus on the processes and structures that reinforce inequalities between women/girls and men/boys. Many see these inequalities as a cost to society as a whole. Others use a rights based approach recognising that women and girls are denied their human rights because they are women. Specific focus on promoting the rights of women and girls is therefore seen as necessary to redress the balance.

The success of your campaign lies in how and where power is exercised in your organisation. If you are able to transform the seats of power then in effect you have moved your campaign to a position of success.

Set your campaign goals to focus on the change for women in the workplace. For example, if attitudes and social norms are going to be a major barrier, then your objectives should look, at least in part, at ways to change attitudes or to increase marginalised women's own sense of power. Look at the strategic interests of women and this will be used to inform your campaign goals. Remembering that deeply entrenched power relations lie behind gender inequality, your strategy should reflect and promote strong women's rights and values.

In the messaging of your campaigns you must seek to challenge the stereotypes associated with communication. Women are too often pitied as victims or alternatively idealised as heroes. Both are problematic. Presenting mothers as heroes can be particularly difficult as it undermines women's rights by suggesting that they are happy with their load. Try to present a more honest and rounded picture. Stereotypes of women as carers are also presented again and again. Be creative – you could try some images of men in non-traditional roles and may find that this is inspirational to your audience. Also think about how you describe women and particularly about whether you're using gendered adjectives ('dainty' and 'bossy' are just two, but there are many).[168]

Always #LikeAGirl[169]

A social experiment was conducted to change the idea of the age old phrase #LikeAGirl, which is usually taken in a negative light. The idea was to convert this very term into something that represents strength, talent, character, and positivity.

One of the most sought-over campaigns, that garnered global appreciation, the P&G feminine care brand included adolescent girls to put out this message.

You therefore have to strategise and implement a campaign that is suitable for your audience. You cannot rely on national campaigns on gender equality, which are usually isolated to Women's Month, to ensure the success of your gender equality initiatives. A 20-year review was commissioned to the Human Sciences Research Council (HSRC) to look at the progress made on gender equality since the establishment of CGE in 1996. Amongst the projects and studies that the Gender Commission has conducted include: Gender Transformation at the Institutions of Higher Learning, Gender Transformation in the Private and Public Sector, the African Gender Development Index (AGDI) study, Policy Dialogues with various Policy Makers both in the Public and Private Sector. This is in addition to the large-scale outreach and legal clinics that the Legal and Public and Education Information Departments conduct to raise awareness, and to monitor and evaluate the extent of gender transformation in the country.[170] These studies have discovered that on reflection, South Africa should be commended on its attempt to acknowledge women's equality in its policies and legislative framework. The lack of change thereof is a result of the misalignment between legislative priorities and implementation. South Africa needs to do more work towards making these policies a reality for women. The 'work' is really everyone's responsibility and starts with you in your organisation. The value of a targeted campaign cannot be stressed enough as the key means of ensuring that a message becomes embedded in the psyche of your employees.

Like the late, great Kofi Annan once said:

> "Gender equality is more than a goal in itself. It is a precondition for meeting the challenge of reducing poverty, promoting sustainable development and building good governance".

The McKinsey Global Institute concluded that if women and men played an identical role in the labour market, it could add a further US$28 trillion to global annual gross domestic product (GDP) by 2025.[171] The inclusion of women as equal players in the labour force cannot be disputed. The report *Better Leadership, Better World: Women Leading for the Global Goals* by #WomenRising2018, an initiative launched by the Business Sustainable and Development Commission, shows that women's leadership can unlock major opportunities linked to sustainable economy.

Benefits of Gender Equality in the Workplace[172]

★ Companies where women accounted for at least 15 percent of senior management, had 18 percent higher profitability than companies with fewer women in senior management.

★ Companies with a high degree of gender equality, performed 11 percent better than companies with a lower level of gender equality. These companies also performed better than the general market in the same period, while companies with low levels of gender equality lost ground.

★ Managers who included women had lower bankruptcy risk than other companies, and there was a greater likelihood of managing decisions that gave significant long-term profitability and success.

Changing culture, people's values, or making big social changes is not done by regulation, policies or by writing new laws alone, but it is a way to facilitate and ensure that changes are possible. Your campaign can also be sustained by hosting "Lunch on the Lawn" where you use these platforms to ensure that constant messaging is reinforced through speakers' testimonies. There are a plethora of organisations who will provide you with speakers who may come to inspire your employees in short 'punchy' sessions without the formal training programme attendance. The latter is important but is not the only means of ensuring that your campaigns are successful. The aim here is to change mindsets.

This chapter discussed the use of campaigns as a long-term strategy to intrinsically change the way in which staff think about and accept gender mainstreaming as a transformation strategy for gender equality. These campaigns can be adapted given the size of your organisation and must take into consideration the elements of culture, media, etc described above.

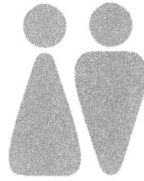

CHAPTER 10

Where to now?

It is necessary to recognise the workplace as a space that is charged with emotions, cultures, prejudices, etc. The workplace is not a gender-neutral space. As a Human Resources practitioner, you are implementing a solution for transformation related to gender equality. This cannot be located on its own and therefore must also take into account other issues of diversity. Gender issues in an organisation are not always visible – some are tacit and will need to be unearthed through undertaking a gender audit. A visible indicator could be, for example, the representation of women at levels of an organisation. However, this is not an apt reflection of the gendered barriers. Sexual harassment may exist but may not be as visible due to fears around victimisation.

Gender equality and ultimately transformation in your institution is everyone's responsibility. However, it is necessary to reflect on Chapter 2 when implementing gender mainstreaming as a strategy. The ultimate goal of using gender mainstreaming as a strategy is to achieve gender equality in the organisation. You must undertake the phases of planning, implementation and consolidation. The consolidation phase is ultimately the main goal wherein gender equality is part of all regular procedures. At this stage, there is no need to apply specific gender mainstreaming methods because gender equality has been merged into the organisation's standard procedures. It is an unquestioned requirement, similar to other principles such as saving costs or working efficiently. Gender equality is sustainably anchored within an organisation's culture.[173] This is easier said than done but ultimately this is the stage which is the ultimate goal.

Promoting equal access opportunities for women is not equivalent to gender mainstreaming. However, it must be included as part of the overall activities to ensure equality in the workplace. Some quick wins that you can explore are:

1. Consider developing equal opportunity policies such as bursaries available to all employees regardless of age and/or vocation. Equal opportunities allow for a more equitable workplace.

2. Including a gender perspective in the organisational activities will result in fresh perspectives on procedures and working results.

3. Place a stronger focus on impacts and results. For example, taking into account differentiated statistics as well as knowledge about gender issues in the planning stages requires a research-based approach to thinking and acting.

4. Introduce new forms of cross-sectoral cooperation and networks within an administration system as well as cooperation between experts and researchers. This can make working routines more interesting.

Notably you must engage the seats of power in enabling your strategy for gender mainstreaming. Often agents of change are those who already subscribe to the way of thinking that you are advocating. Use these agents of change in assisting you to mainstream your strategy in your organisation. As a Human Resource practitioner, the onus is on you to develop the acceptance of gender mainstreaming as a strategy for transformation in your organisation from the highest level. Gender mainstreaming is a top-down approach with senior management leading by example. Noting that the accountability for transformation lies at all levels of the organisation, it is still very important for senior management to lead the process.

As stated earlier, at the current rate of progress, the Global Index for Women indicates that we will only reach the desired outcome of gender equality in 100 years. It is therefore our responsibility to ensure that the timeframe is moved by moving the goal posts. Gender mainstreaming as a strategy for gender equality must be prioritised for its implementation in achieving global success.

As a Human Resource practitioner, it is your responsibility to create or influence the enabling conditions for gender equality in the workplace. Strive to attain a workplace that fosters the value of gender equality and leads initiatives that will assist in embedding this value. Consider the mainstreaming of policies such as flexible time, maternity periods for men and women, and look at targeted capacity-building interventions. Notably you must look at practical interventions to promote the implementation of policies, as discussed earlier, through the mainstreaming of targets in performance agreements from top management to operational staff.

Helena Traschel on weforum.org comments that there are six concrete ways of promoting gender equality at every stage of the hiring and promotion process. As was discussed in Chapter 2, the main failure of gender equality begins at the outset of careers, with men being favoured for appointment and promotion.

1. Rethink job interviews. The question: "What do you think your salary should be?" should be abolished altogether, as women consistently ask for less than men. Instead, interviewers should provide a fair and transparent salary range and ask applicants to position themselves within it.

2. Make gender equality part of training and education. Young people should be supported in choosing jobs that are future-oriented and promising, regardless of their gender.

3. Be proactive about welcoming women. Companies should clearly state that they want to hire, support and promote women. Salaries and promotions should be monitored and evaluated on a regular basis to ensure equal treatment.

4. Make flexibility and work-life balance a part of the wider company culture. Too often, employees have to specifically ask to work part-time or work from home, which can be awkward. Companies should instead offer a broad range of different options.

5. Don't limit your talent pool. Companies should aim for a 50/50 gender split in all their teams – right up to the executive floor. Offering practical support such as childcare, is part of this, as is the right attitude. It should not be a career killer for a man to ask for extended leave because he wants to look after his children.

6. Use the power of networking. Networking, mentoring and coaching opportunities can help women build confidence and develop their careers.[174]

Expert commentary: Jewell Parkinson, Head of Human Resources, SAP, featured in the *Forbes Women, Leadership and Vision* series.[175]

Part of the responsibilities of a Human Resources officer at a global technology company is to ensure we attract, hire, develop and train the best people in all markets, both men and women. Like many technology companies, SAP sees the value of creating and sustaining an environment where diverse talent, including women, can thrive in all functions, across all markets, in all roles and at all levels including leadership.

Parkinson also explains her six steps to a successful and sustainable diverse workplace that encourages gender equality. These echo the sentiments of this book by reinforcing the importance of key elements in the implementation of gender mainstreaming strategies for gender equality.

"People and their talents are among the core drivers of sustainable, long-term economic growth. If half of these talents are underdeveloped or underutilised, growth and sustainability will be compromised. Moreover, there is a compelling and fundamental values case for empowering women: women represent one half of the global population – they deserve equal access to health, education, earning power and political representation".[176]

The workplace requires various interventions to ensure transformation. Consider the following:

★ Workplaces to provide equal pay for work of equal or comparable value.

★ The removal of barriers to the full and equal participation of women in the workforce.

★ Access to all occupations and industries, including leadership roles, regardless of gender.

★ The elimination of discrimination on the basis of gender, particularly in relation to family and caring responsibilities. Achieving gender equality is important for workplaces not only because it is 'fair' and 'the right thing to do,' but because it is also linked to a country's overall economic performance.

If these conditions are set up, an enabling environment begins to emerge. Workplace gender equality is associated with[177]:

★ Improved national productivity and economic growth.

★ Future proofing the Australian economy.

★ Increased organisational performance.

★ Enhanced ability of companies to attract talent and retain employees.

★ Enhanced organisational reputation.

The case of Australia

Goldman Sachs & JB Were calculated that the rise in female employment since 1974 has boosted Australian economic activity by 22%.[178] Projections by KPMG indicate that if the labour force participation gap between men and women was halved, Australia's annual GDP would increase by $60 billion in just 20 years. Our cumulative living standards would also rise by $140 billion in this time.[179]

Research conducted by the Diversity Council of Australia shows that flexible working arrangements are important to female and male employees of all ages.[180] Research also suggests a positive association between flexibility for men and commitment to work, with flexibility being one of the top five employment drivers for men.[181] Flexible working arrangements enable employees to meet their family as well as their personal needs and evidence suggests that all employees including the young, the senior, and employees with family responsibilities are all more likely to be engaged and motivated in workplaces with access to flexible working arrangements.[182]

The case of Australia points to the need to focus on increased organisational performance. A diverse and inclusive workforce, regardless of size and industry, generates tangible benefits, such as increased efficiency, productivity, innovation, creativity and improved employee engagement. A diverse workforce tends to produce a more holistic analysis of the issues an organisation faces and spurs greater effort and motivation, leading to improved decision-making.[183]

The correlation between more female leaders in top leadership positions and increased financial profitability was also evident in an analysis of the performance of 21,980 firms in 2014 in 91 countries by the Peterson Institute for International Economics.[184] Diverse teams are associated with greater innovative capacity for an organisation. International research examining gender-diverse teams suggests that more gender-balanced teams are better in promoting an environment where innovation can flourish compared to teams of one particular gender.[185]

As a Human Resources practitioner, the correlation described by Noland, Moran and Kotschwar is notable. Diverse teams must be fostered and also supported in order to promote an innovative environment. Having gender equality isn't just an important issue for women; workplace gender equality is also directly related to the overall economic performance of corporations and in general, the whole country. Studies show that where there is greater workplace equality there is[186]:

★ Better national economic growth.

★ Increased national productivity.

★ Stronger reputations for organisations built upon fairness and equal rights.

★ Increased inflow of highly qualified candidates for jobs.

★ Better overall organisational performance in corporations.

How to achieve gender equality in the workplace[187]

For organisations serious about improving gender equality in the workplace, here are a few things that can be done:

1. Diversify the training process

    Training is essential at all levels of an organisation for employees to become educated about the advantages of gender equality. This helps to reduce gender biases and stereotypes.

2. Foster all-inclusive work environments

    Encourage women to enter fields which may have traditionally been male dominated and eliminate hostility in the workplace.

3. Encourage mentorships

    Women in leadership roles can play a huge role in inspiring and recruiting other talented and driven women.

Gender inequality is a problem that many women still face in the workplace. The best way to eradicate this problem is to increase awareness about its existence in order to dispel any lingering gender biases which may exist. Once that is done, strides can be made towards offering women the same opportunities, salaries, and positions as their male counterparts.

As a Human Resource practitioner you may want to also explore the use of positive reinforcement. This must be encouraged as a leadership practice at all levels. Earlier, I discussed the importance of values-based leadership and explained some practical strategies for enforcing values-based leadership in the workplace. Notably, the use of positive reinforcement can assist in embedding the principles of values-based leadership. A recent *Harvard Business Review* article reported that positive reinforcement actually motivates employees better than punishment. Not only is it more effective at motivating change, but it's also less damaging to the employer-employee relationship. This practice must be exercised when targets are met for gender equality in the workplace and where it is evident that gender equality has been inculcated in organisational operations.

Jeff Miller, the senior director of talent management at Cornerstone OnDemand, said he once changed jobs because he regularly received negative reinforcement. In environments like the one Miller described, attrition is common because employees feel that their boss doesn't trust them.

Creating trust in the workplace is a difficult task to succeed at. One is never certain as to how long it will take for the trust in the workplace to be built. However, the recognition for work well done and decisions well taken means that employees feel validated and therefore trust begins to be built. Positive reinforcement is the practice of rewarding desirable employee behaviour in order to strengthen that behaviour. For example, when you praise an employee for doing a good job, you increase the likelihood of him/her doing that job very well again. Positive reinforcement both shapes behaviour and enhances an employee's self-image.

Recognising and rewarding desirable employee behaviour is the essential key to motivating employees to work more productively. This method will reap many benefits[188]:

1. It clearly defines and communicates expected behaviours and strengthens the connection between high performance and rewards.

2. It reinforces an employee's behaviour immediately after learning a new technique and promotes quick, thorough learning.

3. It motivates effective workers to continue to do good work. Lack of reinforcement leads to job dissatisfaction.

4. It increases productivity by rewarding workers who conserve time and materials.

5. Employees who are rewarded after they successfully perform feel self-confident and become eager to learn new techniques, take advanced training, and accept more responsibility.

6. Rewarding employees who suggest improved work procedures will produce more innovation – if you create a relaxed work environment, reward new ideas and tolerate innovative failures.

7. Employees who receive recognition for their achievements are more enthusiastic about their work, more cooperative, and more open to change.

8. When you show appreciation and reward employees for good work, you increase their job commitment and organisational loyalty.

Guidelines for Positive Reinforcement[189]

These guidelines will help make your reinforcements most effective:

★   Be specific.

★   Give the employee concrete, specific information about what he/she did right.

★   Reinforce immediately.

★   Reward the employee as soon as possible after his/her good behaviour.

★   Be sincere.

★   Show genuine appreciation for the employee's achievement.

★   Reinforce often but unpredictably.

★   Regular reinforcement comes to be expected and fails to motivate. Frequent, but random, reinforcement is more effective.

★   Reward small increments of improvement.

★   Most performance improvement is gradual. Rewarding good effort and small improvements will lead to bigger improvements.

★   Give realistic reinforcement.

★   Rewards should be proportionate to the importance of the behaviour.

★   Personalise the reinforcement.

These guidelines can be mainstreamed into the training offered to senior management and those in a supervisory position to embed the culture of positivity in the workplace and thus create an enabling environment for the uptake of gender mainstreaming as a strategy for gender equality.

🧳 The Case of Sears Department Store in Pennsylvania[190]

In 2006, a branch manager of a Sears Department Store in Pennsylvania was having a difficult time getting his staff to prompt customers to apply for Sears credit cards. Customers had continually said "No" whenever asked, and this negative reinforcement had resulted in the employees no longer trying. The branch manager decided to try a different approach using reinforcement methods to motivate employees. He offered his employees a bonus on their paycheck for every credit card application processed. Every 90 days, the employee with the most submitted applications would be recognised at work and receive a gift card. In addition to the positive reinforcement, he also made it clear any employee who did not submit at least five applications a month would be required to complete training to improve their productivity. While his employees were motivated by the positive reinforcements, the training worked to ensure no employee was allowed to slack off. As a result, the Sears store became the number one store for credit card applications in the state.

The manager in this case study created an entire rewards system for his employees. While this is a great thing to do, positive reinforcement doesn't always have to be on such a large scale. A simple pat on the back or thank-you note serves as an everyday form of positive reinforcement.

Coaches from Forbes Coaches Council offer some tangible solutions to promote gender equality in the workplace:

1. Have In-house Champions

Over the years, gender equality issues have been present in many workplaces. The good news is that women are becoming more and more empowered in the corporate world these days. In fact, an article in CNN states that "companies with a high representation of women board members significantly outperformed those with no female directors". In other words, the more diverse leaders are on the topic, the better the rate of success. My advice is to promote gender equality in the office by creating a group of in-house advocates. Having employees who champion this advocacy means they can oversee short-term, and sustain long-term, actions towards equality. *–Dr. Cherry Collier, Personality Matters, INC.*

2. Be Transparent About Wanting to Make a Change

The easiest way is to look inside your organisation and answer the following: How many women do you employ? How many of those women are in top level/executive positions? Are women in equivalent roles to men paid equally? If you're serious about promoting female equality in the workplace, be transparent about your desire to address these questions and then follow up with real, shared action. *–Cha Tekeli, Chalamode, Inc.*

3. Acknowledge and Reward Different Leadership Styles

Men and women lead in different ways. Men are comfortable with hierarchy and tend to promote themselves and their individual work. Women lead in democratic, consensus-building ways, advocate for their teams and don't stand out as individual leaders. Hence, adding group accomplishments and team productivity into performance evaluations will reward women's collaborative leadership styles. *–Julie P. Kantor, Ph.D., JP Kantor Consulting*

4. Implement Three Simple Steps

I believe these three steps will help us reach female equality in the workplace more quickly:

1. Remove names from the resumé screening process and select candidates for interviews based only on education, experience and other required qualifications.

2. Pay people market-rate salaries versus making salary decisions based on salary history.

3. Change company culture to reward outcomes achieved, not hours worked. *–Anu Mandapati, IMPACT Leadership for Women*

5. Know Your Bias

Men in the workplace need to intimately examine and come to peace with the fact that they are innately biased — if not deliberately and maliciously, then passively and subconsciously. Men, let's level with one another. We don't know how to be perfectly unbiased, and no human being is. Admitting bias (if only to yourself) is the best step to being more open, objective and honest in the workplace. *-Dave Ursillo, The Literati Writers*

6. Have Open and Candid Dialogs Between Men and Women

Too often, women speak almost exclusively with other women about this issue. Too often, men speak about it far too little — and rarely with women. If you're a man, make it a point to discuss this with women openly, and do your best not to take it personally. If you're a woman, make a point of talking to men about this, doing your best to leave any blame/judgement you may be feeling out of it. *-Dan Kimble, Resonance Executive Coaching*

7. Encourage Women to Make the Leap

So many women miss out on great opportunities because they mistakenly believe they are underqualified. Meanwhile, men often go after promotions and projects they are not qualified for. Here is a great opening for companies to help even the playing field: Actively encourage women to take more chances and go for opportunities they desire. External support is great for confidence-building. *-Laura Garnett, Garnett Consulting LLC*

8. Build New Roles for Women so Business Can Evolve for the Better

Times have changed and it's time to change "business as usual". Women bring a different and unique perspective to business and we need to celebrate and integrate it. Instead of trying to shove women into the roles that men have been doing for decades, we should be more interested in hiring savvy women to develop new roles and benchmarks for how success is created. *- Brett Baughman, The Brett Baughman Companies, Inc.*

9. Stop Pay Disparity and the Gender Gap

In order to promote female equality in the workplace, it must first begin with equal pay. Pay disparity and the gender gap are two of the biggest recurring issues in the workforce, and certainly a catalyst to ongoing class action lawsuits. Paying employees fairly and equally based on experience level, not on gender, is truly the first step needed to properly promote gender equality. *–Wendi Weiner, JD, NCRW, CPRW, CCTC, CCM, The Writing Guru*

10. Commit to Three Objectives

Workplace gender dynamics have come a long way since the 1980s, and we have a long way to go. In my opinion, three things could significantly promote gender equality in the workplace:

1. Equal pay for equal work.

2. Childcare options and flexible hours.

3. Outstanding mentoring programmes for high-potential women leaders.

Companies that commit to these objectives will have a serious competitive advantage. *–Dr Priya Nalkur-Pai*

11. Start at the Top

For real equality to happen, requires a shift in organisational culture, which typically starts at the top of the company chain of command. Create a cross-functional team to study the current culture and present to execs what other companies – competitors and non-competitors alike – are doing to promote female equality and the positive effects on culture, retention and bottom line. *– Emily Kapit, MS, MRW, ACRW, CPRW, ReFresh Your Step, LLC*

12. Have More Options for Women

The disparity in pay generally occurs when a woman decides to start a family. At that point, women may less actively seek more demanding roles due to family obligations. Companies need to create more flexible options for women including telecommuting, job shares and consulting assignments to motivate women and keep financial and professional continuity intact. *–Barbara Safani, Career Solvers*

13. Walk It Out in Daily Life

It goes beyond our workplace to our home life, too. What we teach our young girls and women about who they are and how they can contribute starts early. Walking it out in our actions and communications removes fear and creates places for change, including the current workplace. *– Jen Kelchner, TeenTrep.co*

These experts provide a look into the necessary interventions for success with gender equality in the workplace. Notably, these aspects have been discussed in detail in previous chapters and can be adapted to your organisation depending on the size and project needs.

Conclusion

Several pieces of local, regional and international legislation have been put in place to ensure that the workplace is regulated and that gender quality is understood as a major priority. The legislation is but one element that addresses a much larger problem. This book offers practical solutions for Human Resource practitioners and those working seeking to implement a transformation strategy in the workplace, to implement initiatives that will ensure gender equality in the workplace. I have emphasised various aspects in this book and will reiterate that gender mainstreaming is a strategy for gender equality, a transformation strategy that must be led from the top-down.

Human Resource practitioners must engage senior management for their buy-in for any initiative to succeed. The success of this aspect will result in many operational projects finding momentum. The importance of values-based leadership for managers at senior level has also been stressed as a major component of the gender mainstreaming strategy. Managers must see themselves as leaders who must embody the values set down for their organisation. If you are able to succeed in at least beginning this process, then that in itself is a major accomplishment. Change is slow and realistic targets must be set in your gender action plan. The latter is the key to mainstreaming gender for gender equality. Managers and employees at all levels must commit to these goals/targets in their performance agreements and relevant project plans to ensure that gender equality is met as an overall organisational goal.

The availing of the necessary resources and the creation of an enabling environment will only be sustained through the concerted efforts of constant messaging and campaigning to internal clients (namely staff members). This book offers practical insights and it is hoped that it will offer you some practical guidance as to how to achieve gender equality in your workplace.

Endnotes

1   Krivkovich, A., Robinson, K., Starikova, I., Valentino, R. & Yee, L. (2017). *Women in the Workplace 2017*. McKinsey & Company. Available at: https://www.mckinsey.com/featured-insights/gender-equality/women-in-the-workplace-2017 (Accessed 10 April 2019).

2   Lanvin, B. & Monteiro, F. (2019). The Global Talent Competitiveness Index 2019: Entrepreneurial Talent and Global Competitiveness. Insead. Available at: https://www.insead.edu/sites/default/files/assets/dept/globalindices/docs/GTCI-2019-Report.pdf Accessed 10 March 2019).

3   Stats SA. (2017). *Quarterly Labour Force Survey, Quarter 2: 2017*. Available at: https://www.statssa.gov.za/publications/P0211/P02112ndQuarter2017.pdf (Accessed 11 April 2019).

4   Pivot Point. (2017). *Five Questions to Ask to get a Gender Equality Conversation Started in Your Organization*. 2015 Available at: https://www.nextpivotpoint.com/five-questions-ask-get-gender-equality-conversation-started-organization/ (Accessed 10 April 2019).

5   Krivkovich, A., Nadeau, M., Robinson, K., Robinson, N., Starikova, I. & Yee, L. (2018). *Women in the Workplace 2018*. McKinsey. Available at: https://www.mckinsey.com/featured-insights/gender-equality/women-in-the-workplace-2018 (Accessed: 10 May 2019).

6   Reference.com. (n.d.). *What is the difference between diversity and equality?* Available at: https://www.reference.com/world-view/difference-between-diversity-equality-251a899d54de3637 (Accessed: 9 May 2019).

7   SGBA e-Learning Resource: Rising to the Challenge. (2009). *Distinguishing between equity and equality*. Available at: http://sgba-resource.ca/en/concepts/equity/distinguish-between-equity-and-equality/ (Accessed 8 May 2019).

8   Lazzari, Z. (2019). *Definition of equality in the Workplace*. Available at: https://smallbusiness.chron.com/definition-equality-workplace-14653.html (Accessed 7 May 2019).

9   Adams, J. (2014). *Men as Agents for Change*. Policy seminar, Government Equalities Office. June 2014. Presentation.

10 Hays. (2014). *5 Benefits of implementing a gender diversity policy in the workplace*. Available at: https://www.hays.be/en/career-academy/diversity/5-benefits-of-implementing-a-gender-diversity-policy-in-the-workplace-1978766 (Accessed: 4 May 2019).

11 The Hague Academy for Local Governance. (2019). *How to Systematically Improve Gender Equality in your Organisation*. Available at: https://thehagueacademy.com/blog/2019/02/systematically-improve-gender-equality-organisation/ (Accessed 13 April 2019).

12   Fong, M.S., Wakeman, W. & Bhushan, A. (1996). Toolkit on Gender in Water and Sanitation, the World Bank, Washington, D.C. Available at: http://www. worldbank.org/gender/know/water.pdf (Accessed on 27 March 2019).

13   Onley, D. (2016). *HR Key in Helping Employers Achieve Gender Equality*. SHRM. Available at: https://www.shrm.org/hr-today/news/hr-magazine/1116/ pages/hr-key-in-helping-organizations-achieve-gender-equality.aspx (Accessed 19 April 2019).

14   United Nations Population Fund (UNFPA). (2009). *UNFPA Annual Report 2009*, p1. Available at: https://www.unfpa.org/sites/default/files/pub-pdf/annual_ report_09.pdf (Accessed 20 April 2019).

15   United Nations Population Fund (UNFPA). (2009). *UNFPA Annual Report 2009*, p2. Available at: https://www.unfpa.org/sites/default/files/pub-pdf/annual_ report_09.pdf (Accessed 20 April 2019).

16   Reeves, H. & Baden, S. (2000). *Gender and Development: Concepts and Definitions*. Prepared for the Department for International Development (DFID). University of Sussex, p12.

17   United Nations Women. (2019). *Short History of the Commission on the Status of Women*. Available at: http://www.unwomen.org/en/digital-library/ publications/2019/02/a-short-history-of-the-commission-on-the-status-of-women (Accessed 20 April 2019).

18   United Nations Women. (2001). Gender Mainstreaming: Strategy for Promoting Gender Equality, p2. Office of the Special Advisor on Gender Issues and the Advancement of Women. Available at: https://www.un.org/womenwatch/ osagi/pdf/factsheet1.pdf (Accessed 20 April 2019).

19   United Nations. (2002). *Gender Mainstreaming: An Overview*. Available at: https:// www.un.org/womenwatch/osagi/pdf/e65237.pdf Accessed 19 April 2019.

20   Ministry of Foreign Affairs, Foreign Information and Communication, the Netherlands. (2002). *Institutional and Organisational Change: a) Gender mainstreaming*, 1. Available at: https://antifeministpraxis.files.wordpress. com/2017/05/institutionalchange-gendermainstreaming.pdf. (Accessed 10 March 2019).

21   European Institute for Gender Equality. (n.d.). Institutional Transformation: What is institutional transformation. Available at: https://eige.europa.eu/ gender-mainstreaming/toolkits/gender-institutional-transformation/what-institutional-transformation Accessed: 10 April 2019

22   Schooley, S. (2019). *SWOT Analysis: What it is and When to use it*. Available at: https:// www.businessnewsdaily.com/4245-swot-analysis.html (Accessed 30 April 2019).

23   Schooley, S. (2019). *SWOT Analysis: What it is and When to use it*. Available at: https:// www.businessnewsdaily.com/4245-swot-analysis.html (Accessed 30 April 2019).

24   Schooley, S. (2019). *SWOT Analysis: What it is and When to use it*. Available at: https:// www.businessnewsdaily.com/4245-swot-analysis.html (Accessed 30 April 2019).

25 European Institute for Gender Equality. (n.d.). Institutional Transformation: What is institutional transformation? Available at: https://eige.europa.eu/gender-mainstreaming/toolkits/gender-institutional-transformation/what-institutional-transformation (Accessed: 23 April 2019)

26 Hassim, S. (1999) 'From presence to power: women's citizenship in a new democracy'. *Agenda*. 40: 6-17

27 Department Women, Children and People with Disabilities, p11. (2014). South Africa's Beijing +20 Report. Available at: http://pmg-assets.s3-website-eu-west-1.amazonaws.com/150908review_Beijing20.pdf (Accessed: 23 April 2019)

28 United Nations. (1995). 'Beijing Platform for Action', p12. New York. Available at: http://www.un.org/womenwatch (Accessed 01 February 2019).

29 Wilson, S. (2005). Young African Women Mobilising. *Agenda Feminist Media*, p64.

30 Julien, L. & Majake, C. (2005). Empowering Women for Gender Equity: Beyond Beijing. *Agenda*, 64(78).

31 Moletsane, R. (2005). Looking back, looking forward: Analysing gender equality in South African education 10 years after Beijing. *Agenda*. 64:80-88.

32 Grant (2005)

33 Van der Westhuizen, B. (2005). *South African Human Resource Management for the Public Sector*. Pretoria: Juta and Company Ltd.

34 Ikechukwu, U.B. & Chukwuemeka, E.E.O. (2013). 'The obstacles to effective policy implementation by the Public Bureaucracy in developing nations: The case of Nigeria'. *Kuwait Chapter of Arabian Journal of Business and Management Review*. 2(7): 59-68.

35 Roux, N.L. (2002). 'Public policy-making and policy analysis in South Africa amidst transformation, change and globalisation: Views on participants and role-players in the policy analytic procedure'. *Journal of Public Administration*. 37(4): 418-437.

36 Roux, N.L. (2002). 'Public policy-making and policy analysis in South Africa amidst transformation, change and globalisation: Views on participants and role-players in the policy analytic procedure'. *Journal of Public Administration*. 37(4): 418-437.

37 Johnsson-Latham, G. (2004). 'Gender Mainstreaming: The Second-Best Option'. *Spotlight* (3): 5-6.

38 Alston, M. (2006). 'Gender Mainstreaming in Practice: A View from Rural Australia'. *National Women's Studies Association Journal*. 18(2): 123-129.

39 Hannan, C. (2000). 'From Concept to Action: Gender Mainstreaming in Operational Activities'. Paper delivered at the Technical Review Meeting: Assessment of Gender Mainstreaming and Empowerment of Women in Sub-Saharan Africa, UN Headquarters, New York, 20-21.

40   Leyenaar, M. (2004). *Political Empowerment of Women: The Netherlands and Other Countries*. Leiden: Martinues Nijhoff Publishers, p210.

41   Wendoh, S. & Wallace, T. (2005). 'Re-thinking Gender Mainstreaming in African NGOs and Communities'. *Gender and Development*. 13(2): 70-73.

42   Lyons, T., Curnow, J. & Mather, G. (2004). 'Developing Gender Mainstreaming and "Gender Respect". Development Bulletin. (64): 37-41.

43   Moser, C. & Moser, A. (2005). 'Gender Mainstreaming since Beijing, a review of limitations of international institutions'. *Gender and Development*. 13(2), pp576-590.

44   IDASA Working Paper. (2004). Democracy without people: Political institutions and Citizenship in the New South Africa, p22-23. Available at: http://afrobarometer.org/sites/default/files/publications/Working%20paper/AfropaperNo82.pdf (Accessed 1 March 2019).

45   Clisby, S. (2005). Gender mainstreaming or just more male-streaming? *Gender & Development*. 13. 23-35.

46   Riley, B. (2004). Public Sector Reform Programmes and Performance Management in Trinidad and Tobago. A Country Position Paper, p11. Available at: http://unpan1.un.org/intradoc/groups/public/documents/caricad/unpan017179.pdf. (Accessed 5 March 2019).

47   Post, L.A., Raile, L.N. & Raile, E.D. (2010). 'Defining Political Will'. *Politics & Policy*. 38(4): 653-676.

48   Post, L.A., Raile, L.N. & Raile, E.D. (2010). 'Defining Political Will'. *Politics & Policy*. 38(4): 653-676.

49   Kapoutsis, I., Treadway, D.C. & Bentley, J. (2015). 'Measuring Political Will in Organisations: Theoretical Construct Development and Empirical Validation'. *Journal of Management*. 43 (7): 2252-2279.

50   Rokeach, M. (1973). *The nature of human values*. New York: Free Press; Schwartz, S. H. (1996). Value priorities & Behavior: Applying a theory of integrated value systems. In C. Seligman, J. M. Olson & M. P. Zanna (Eds.), The Ontario symposium: Vol. 8. *The psychology of values* (pp. 1-24). Hillsdale, NJ: Lawrence Erlbaum; Knafo, A. & Schwartz, S.H. (2001). Value socialization in families of Israeli-born and Soviet-born adolescents in Israel, *Journal of Cross-Cultural Psychology*, 32(2), 213- 28.

51   Eysenck, H. (1954). The Psychology of Politics. Available at: http://uspp.csbsju.edu/resources/preface.html. (Accessed on 17 March 2019.); Rokeach, M. (1973). *The nature of human values*. New York: Free Press; Schwartz, S.H. (1992). 'Universals in the content and structure of values: Theoretical advances and empirical tests in 20 countries'. *Advances in Experimental Social Psychology*. 25: 1-65.

52   Mind Tools Team. (2019). 'What are your Values?'. Available at: https://www.mindtools.com/pages/article/newTED_85.htm (Accessed 10 January 2019).

53   Schwartz, S.H. (1992). 'Universals in the content and structure of values: Theoretical advances and empirical tests in 20 countries'. *Advances in Experimental Social Psychology*. 25: 1-65.

54   Schmidt, T.M., & Møller, A.L. (n.d.). Stereotypical Barriers for Women in Management. Available at: http://pure.au.dk/portal/files/36185535/opgave_til_nettet.pdf (Accessed 23 April 2019).

55   Krivkovich, A., Nadeau, M., Robinson, K., Robinson, N., Starikova, I. & Yee, L. (2018). *Women in the Workplace 2018*. McKinsey. Available at: https://www.mckinsey.com/featured-insights/gender-equality/women-in-the-workplace-2018 (Accessed: 10 May 2019).

56   Krivkovich, A., Nadeau, M., Robinson, K., Robinson, N., Starikova, I. & Yee, L. (2018). *Women in the Workplace 2018*. McKinsey. Available at: https://www.mckinsey.com/featured-insights/gender-equality/women-in-the-workplace-2018 (Accessed: 10 May 2019).

57   Krivkovich, A., Nadeau, M., Robinson, K., Robinson, N., Starikova, I. & Yee, L. (2018). *Women in the Workplace 2018*. McKinsey. Available at: https://www.mckinsey.com/featured-insights/gender-equality/women-in-the-workplace-2018 (Accessed: 10 May 2019).

58   Krivkovich, A., Nadeau, M., Robinson, K., Robinson, N., Starikova, I. & Yee, L. (2018). *Women in the Workplace 2018*. McKinsey. Available at: https://www.mckinsey.com/featured-insights/gender-equality/women-in-the-workplace-2018 (Accessed: 10 May 2019).

59   United Nations Framework Convention on Climate Change. (2017). *Gender and climate change*. Available at: https://unfccc.int/resource/docs/2017/sbi/eng/l29.pdf (Accessed 21 April 2019).

60   30 Percent Club Southern Africa. (2017). *Best Practices in Gender Mainstreaming*. Available at: http://www.businessengage.co.za/wp-content/uploads/best-practices-july-2017.pdf (Accessed 20 April 2019).

61   30 Percent Club Southern Africa. (2017). *Best Practices in Gender Mainstreaming*. Available at: http://www.businessengage.co.za/wp-content/uploads/best-practices-july-2017.pdf (Accessed 20 April 2019).

62   VicHealth. (2016). Supporting gender equity in the workplace. Available at: http://www.monash.vic.gov.au/files/assets/public/our-services/health-and-safety/gender-equity/supporting-gender-equity-in-the-workplace.pdf (Accessed 29 April 2019).

63   VicHealth. (2016). Supporting gender equity in the workplace. Available at: http://www.monash.vic.gov.au/files/assets/public/our-services/health-and-safety/gender-equity/supporting-gender-equity-in-the-workplace.pdf (Accessed 29 April 2019).

64 Wikipedia. (2019). *Global Gender Gap Report*. Available at: https://en.wikipedia.org/wiki/Global_Gender_Gap_Report (Accessed: 9 May 2019)

65 Mkentane, L. (2017). *Retrogressive SA in top 20 of Africa's gender equal lands*. Business Report. Available at: https://www.iol.co.za/business-report/retrogressive-sa-in-top-20-of-africas-gender-equal-lands-11838213 Accessed 29 April 2019.

66 Rathgeber, M.E. (2006). 'Towards a Gender Action Plan for the Department of Technical Cooperation (TC) International Atomic Energy Agency (IAEA)', p14. Report for the Department of Technical Cooperation, Mexico.

67 Rai, S. M. (2008). *The Gender Politics of Development: Essays in Hope and Despair*. London: Zed, p75.

68 Madrid. S. (2009). 'Silence, Fear and Desire: Why Chile doesn't have a gender equity policy in education, and some lessons for Australia'. Paper presented at the AARE Annual Conference, National Convention Centre, Canberra 29 November – 3 December, 2009.

69 Madrid. S. (2009). 'Silence, Fear and Desire: Why Chile doesn't have a gender equity policy in education, and some lessons for Australia'. Paper presented at the AARE Annual Conference, National Convention Centre, Canberra 29 November – 3 December, 2009.

70 Madrid. S. (2009). 'Silence, Fear and Desire: Why Chile doesn't have a gender equity policy in education, and some lessons for Australia'. Paper presented at the AARE Annual Conference, National Convention Centre, Canberra 29 November – 3 December, 2009.

71 Madrid. S. (2009). 'Silence, Fear and Desire: Why Chile doesn't have a gender equity policy in education, and some lessons for Australia'. Paper presented at the AARE Annual Conference, National Convention Centre, Canberra 29 November – 3 December, 2009.

72 Government of Chile. (2004). Report on Implementation of The Beijing Platform for Action Presented by The Government of Chile to the United Nations Division for The Advancement of Women, p25. Available at: https://www.un.org/womenwatch/daw/Review/responses/CHILE-English.pdf Accessed 22 April 2019.

73 Tanzarn, N. (2003). 'Integrating gender into World Bank financed transport programmes'. Case study of Uganda Road Sector Programme Support.

74 Ratele, K. (2007). 'Native chief and White headman: A critical African gender analysis of culture'. *Agenda*. (72): 77-79.

75 Rathgeber, M.E. (2006). 'Towards a Gender Action Plan for the Department of Technical Cooperation (TC) International Atomic Energy Agency (IAEA)'. Report for the Department of Technical Cooperation, Mexico.

76   Rathgeber, M.E. (2006). 'Towards a Gender Action Plan for the Department of Technical Cooperation (TC) International Atomic Energy Agency (IAEA)'. Report for the Department of Technical Cooperation, Mexico.

77   Rathgeber, M.E. (2006). 'Towards a Gender Action Plan for the Department of Technical Cooperation (TC) International Atomic Energy Agency (IAEA)'. Report for the Department of Technical Cooperation, Mexico.

78   Rathgeber, M.E. (2006). 'Towards a Gender Action Plan for the Department of Technical Cooperation (TC) International Atomic Energy Agency (IAEA)'. Report for the Department of Technical Cooperation, Mexico.

79   Gouws, A. (1999). 'Beyond equality and difference: the politics of women's citizenship'. *Agenda*. 40: 54-58.; Lewis, K. (1999). Communicating Change: Four cases of Quality Programmes. Available at: http://journals.sagepub.com/doi/abs/10.1177/002194360003700201. (Accessed 23 April 2019); and Watson, J. (1997). 'Prioritising women's rights: The Commission on Gender Equality'. *Agenda*. 34: 94-97.

80   Harris, S., Kambon, A. & Clarke, R. (2000). 'Study of Gender Mainstreaming in the Caribbean'. United Nations, p14.

81   Harris, S., Kambon, A. & Clarke, R. (2000). 'Study of Gender Mainstreaming in the Caribbean'. United Nations, p14.

82   Mehra, R. & Gupta, G.T. (2006). 'Gender Mainstreaming: Making it happen'. International Center for Research on Women, 30th Anniversary, p3.

83   The Bureau of Women's Affairs (Gender Affairs) Kingston, Jamaica & The Gender Advisory Committee. (2010). The National Policy for Gender Equality in Jamaica, p19. Available at: https://sta.uwi.edu/igds/documents/JamaicaNPGE-JA-FINALwCover21311.pdf (Accessed 20 January 2019).

84   PWC. (2019). Celebrating International Women's Day: Bold actions for gender equality. Available at: https://www.pwc.com/gx/en/about/diversity/internationalwomensday.html (Accessed 29 April 2019).

85   Worldbank. (2018). The Cost of Gender Inequality: Unrealized Potential: The High Cost Of Gender Inequality in Earnings. Available at: https://www.worldbank.org/en/topic/gender/publication/unrealized-potential-the-high-cost-of-gender-inequality-in-earnings Accessed: 8 May 2019.

86   Wikipedia. (2019). Chapter Nine Institutions (South African Constitution). Available at: https://en.wikipedia.org/wiki/Chapter_nine_institutions (Accessed 28 March 2019).

87   South African Human Rights Commission. (2017). Research Brief on Gender and Equality in South Africa 2013 – 2017. Available at: https://www.sahrc.org.za/home/21/files/RESEARCH%20BRIEF%20ON%20GENDER%20AND%20EQUALITY%20IN%20SOUTH%20AFRICA%202013%20to%202017.pdf Accessed 29 March 2019.

88 Stats SA. (2016). Living Conditions of Households in South Africa 2014/15, p14. Available at: http://www.statssa.gov.za/publications/P0310/P03102014.pdf (Accessed 30 March 2019).

89 Commission for Gender Equality (CGE). (n.d.). About us. Available at: http://www.cge.org.za/about-us/ (Accessed 30 March 2019).

90 Gumede, V. (2008). 'Public policy making in a post-Apartheid South Africa: A preliminary perspective'. *Africanus.* 38(2): 7-23.

91 Busch, J. (2009). Senior Management Support: What is it and why you need it. Available at: http://spendmatters.com/2009/07/29/senior-management-support-what-is-it-and-why-you-need-it/ (Accessed 29 March 2019).

92 Heathfield, S.M. (2019). Executive Support and Leadership in Change Management. Available at: https://www.thebalancecareers.com/executive-support-and-leadership-in-change-management-1917803 (Accessed 29 March 2019).

93 Heathfield, S.M. (2019). Executive Support and Leadership in Change Management. Available at: https://www.thebalancecareers.com/executive-support-and-leadership-in-change-management-1917803 (Accessed 29 March 2019).

94 Heathfield, S.M. (2019). Executive Support and Leadership in Change Management. Available at: https://www.thebalancecareers.com/executive-support-and-leadership-in-change-management-1917803 (Accessed 29 March 2019).

95 Brynard, P.A. (2009). Mapping the factors that influence policy implementation. J. Public Adm., (44) 557-577.

96 DPSA. 2007. Presentation on the head of department's 8-Principle action plan for promoting women's empowerment and gender equality within the Public Service workplace. Available at: http://www.dpsa.gov.za/dpsa2g/documents/networks/hr_forum_10_2007/8-PRINCIPLE.pdf (Accessed 26 March 2019).

97 Boot, A. (2011). Leading Change: What about the Coaching Skills of Senior Leaders. Available at: https://leadershipwatch-aadboot.com/2011/09/27/leading-change-what-about-the-coaching-skills-of-senior-leaders/ (Accessed 29 March 2019).

98 Heathfield, S.M. (2019). Executive Support and Leadership in Change Management. Available at: https://www.thebalancecareers.com/executive-support-and-leadership-in-change-management-1917803 (Accessed 29 March 2019).

99 Workplace Gender Equality Agency. (2013). How to set gender diversity targets. Available at: https://www.wgea.gov.au/sites/default/files/documents/SETTING-GENDER-TARGETS-Online-accessible_0.pdf (Accessed 9 May 2019).

100 Workplace Gender Equality Agency. (2013). How to set gender diversity targets. Available at: https://www.wgea.gov.au/sites/default/files/documents/SETTING-GENDER-TARGETS-Online-accessible_0.pdf (Accessed 9 May 2019).

101 The Glass Hammer. (2015). How Can Values-Based Leadership Improve Your Effectiveness. Available at: https://theglasshammer.com/2015/04/23/how-can-values-based-leadership-improve-your-effectiveness/ (Accessed 27 March 2019).

102 Besharov, M.L., & Khurana, R. *Leading Amidst Competing Technical and Institutional Demands: Revisiting Selznick's Conception of Leadership.* Harvard Business School Working Paper, No. 13-049, November 2012. Available at: https://www.hbs.edu/faculty/Pages/item.aspx?num=43686 (Accessed 29 March 2019).

103 The Glass Hammer. (2015). How Can Values-Based Leadership Improve Your Effectiveness. Available at: https://theglasshammer.com/2015/04/23/how-can-values-based-leadership-improve-your-effectiveness/ (Accessed 27 March 2019).

104 Freifeld, L. (2013). How to build a values-based culture. Available at: https://trainingmag.com/content/how-build-values-based-culture (Accessed 28 March 2019).

105 Freifeld, L. (2013). How to build a values-based culture. Available at: https://trainingmag.com/content/how-build-values-based-culture (Accessed 28 March 2019).

106 Freifeld, L. (2013). How to build a values-based culture. Available at: https://trainingmag.com/content/how-build-values-based-culture (Accessed 28 March 2019).

107 Vinamaki, O.P. (2012) Embedding Value-Based Organisation: An identification of critical success factors and challenges. *The International Journal of Management Science and Information Technology* (IJMSIT), I(3), 37-67, January-March 2012.

108 The Glass Hammer. (2015). How Can Values-Based Leadership Improve Your Effectiveness. Available at: https://theglasshammer.com/2015/04/23/how-can-values-based-leadership-improve-your-effectiveness/ (Accessed 21 April 2019).

109 Krivkovich, A., Nadeau, M., Robinson, K., Robinson, N., Starikova, I. & Yee, L. (2018). *Women in the Workplace 2018.* McKinsey. Available at: https://www.mckinsey.com/featured-insights/gender-equality/women-in-the-workplace-2018 (Accessed: 10 May 2019).

110 Soteres, K. (2018). Advocating for Gender Equality in the Workplace. Available at: https://www.adp.com/spark/articles/2018/04/advocating-for-gender-equality-in-the-workplace.aspx# (Accessed 21 April 2019).

111 VicHealth. (2016). Supporting gender equity in the workplace. Available at: http://www.monash.vic.gov.au/files/assets/public/our-services/health-and-safety/gender-equity/supporting-gender-equity-in-the-workplace.pdf (Accessed 23 April 2019).

112 Commission for Gender Equality (CGE). (2016). CGE report: *M v S, 2016 Mbombela Magistrates Court (Equality Court)*. Available at: http://www.cge.org.za/wp-content/uploads/2014/05/M-v-S-2016-Mbombela-Magistrates-Court-Equality-Court.pdf (Accessed 24 April 2019).

113 Commission for Gender Equality (CGE). (2016). *CGE report: Raedani v M and others 2016 case no 1/2016 Thohoyandou Magistrates Court (Equality Court)* Available at: http://www.cge.org.za/wp-content/uploads/2014/05/Raedani-v-M-and-others.pdf (Accessed 28 April 2019).

114 Commission for Gender Equality (CGE). (2016). *CGE report: National Coalition for Gay and Lesbian Equality and Others v Minister of Home Affairs and Others.* Available at: http://www.cge.org.za/wp-content/uploads/2014/05/National-Coalition-Case-Summary.pdf (Accessed 29 April 2019).

115 Picard, L.A. (2005). The State of the State. Johannesburg: WITS University Press, p13.

116 Fox, W. & Meyer, I.H. (1995). *Public Administration Dictionary*. Johannesburg: Juta Books, p107.

117 Anderson, J.E. (1997). *Public Policy Making*. Boston: Houghton Mifflin, p9.

118 Isaac, L. (n.d.). *Why have policies?* Available at: http://www.leoisaac.com/policy/top126.htm (Accessed 18 April 2019).

119 Gender Equality Cayman Islands. (2012). *Why is gender equality important?* Adapted from: http://genderequality.gov.ky/pledge/why-gender-equality-important (Accessed 10 May 2019).

120 Edigheji, O. (2005). A Democratic Developmental State in Africa? A concept paper research report 105. Available at: https//:www.cps.org.za/cps%20pdf/RR105.pdf. (Accessed on 10 April 2019).

121 Anderson, J.E. (1997). *Public Policy Making*. Boston: Houghton Mifflin.

122 Gruening, G. (1998). Origin and theoretical basis of the New Public Management (NPM). Available at: https://www.inpuma.net/research/papers/salem/gernod.doc. (Accessed 12 April 2019).

123 Boyte, H. (2004). Seeing Like A Democracy: South Africa's Prospects for Global Leadership. *African Journal of Political Science*. Vol 9(1), p4.

124 White, G. (1998). *Constructing a Democratic Developmental State*. In: The Democratic Developmental State: Political and Institutional Design. Robinson, M. & White, G. (Eds.). Oxford: Oxford University Press, p28.

125 Fester, G. (2007). 'Rhetoric or real rights: Gender equality in Africa (1987-2007)'. *Agenda.* 72: 69-180.; Salo, E. (2001) 'Talking about feminisms in Africa'. *Agenda.* (50):58-63.; Salo, E (2007) 'Gendered citizenship, race and women's differentiated access to power in the new South Africa'. *Agenda*, 72, 187-196.; Hassim, S. (1999) 'From presence to power: women's citizenship in a new democracy'. *Agenda.* 40: 6-17; and Govender, P. (2002). 'Farewell speech of Pregs Govender, chairperson of the Joint Monitoring Committee on the Improvement of the Quality of Life and Status of Women in Parliament.'

126 Brynard, P.A. (2009). Mapping the factors that influence policy implementation. J. Public Adm., (44) 557-577.

127 Marshall, C. & Rossman, G.B. (1999). *Designing qualitative research.* London: Sage.

128 National Policy Framework (NPF). (2001). *South Africa's National Policy Framework for Women's Empowerment and Gender Equality*, p8. Available at: https://www.environment.gov.za/sites/default/files/docs/national_policy_framework.pdf (Accessed 18 April 2019).

129 National Policy Framework (NPF). (2001). *South Africa's National Policy Framework for Women's Empowerment and Gender Equality*, p8. Available at: https://www.environment.gov.za/sites/default/files/docs/national_policy_framework.pdf (Accessed 18 April 2019).

130 National Policy Framework (NPF). (2001). *South Africa's National Policy Framework for Women's Empowerment and Gender Equality*, p42. Available at: https://www.environment.gov.za/sites/default/files/docs/national_policy_framework.pdf (Accessed 18 April 2019).

131 National Policy Framework (NPF). (2001). *South Africa's National Policy Framework for Women's Empowerment and Gender Equality*, p45. Available at: https://www.environment.gov.za/sites/default/files/docs/national_policy_framework.pdf (Accessed 18 April 2019).

132 University of California. (1994). *Guide to Writing Policy and Procedure Documents.* Available at: https://policy.ucsc.edu/resources/images/GuidetoWritingPolicy.pdf (Accessed 19 April 2019).

133 The South African Labour Guide. (n.d.). *Code of Good Practice.* Available at: https://www.labourguide.co.za/general/600-code-of-good-practice-on-sexual-harassment113 (Accessed 20 April 2019).

134 The South African Labour Guide. (n.d.). *Code of Good Practice.* Available at: https://www.labourguide.co.za/general/600-code-of-good-practice-on-sexual-harassment113 (Accessed 21 April 2019).

135 South African Kendo Federation. (n.d.). Harassment & Discrimination Policy and Procedures. Available at: https://www.sakf.co.za/CMS/home/harassment-discrimination-policy-and-procedures/ (Accessed 20 April 2019).

136 Walters, H. (1995). *Monitoring and Evaluation from a Gender Perspective. A Guideline.* Netherlands Development Organisation (SNV), Holland.

137 Walters, H. (1995). *Monitoring and Evaluation from a Gender Perspective. A Guideline*. Netherlands Development Organisation (SNV), Holland.

138 Goyder, H., Davies R. & Williamson, W. (1998). *Participatory Impact Assessment. A Report on a DFID Funded ActionAid Research Project on Methods and Indicators for Measuring the Impact of Poverty Reduction*. ActionAid: London.

139 PMG. (2001). National Policy Framework for Women's Empowerment and Gender Equality: Parliament's Gender Conference. Available at: https://pmg.org.za/committee-meeting/10101/. (Accessed 29 April 2019).

140 Goyder, H., Davies R. & Williamson, W. (1998). *Participatory Impact Assessment. A Report on a DFID Funded ActionAid Research Project on Methods and Indicators for Measuring the Impact of Poverty Reduction*. ActionAid: London.

141 Wallace, T. (1998). 'Institutionalizing Gender in UK NGOs'. *Development in Practice*, Vol. 8, No. 2, May 1998, Oxfam: Oxford.

142 European Institute for Gender Equality. (n.d.). *Gender evaluation*. Available at: https://eige.europa.eu/gender-mainstreaming/methods-tools/gender-evaluation (Accessed 20 April 2019).

143 Walters, H. (1995). *Monitoring and Evaluation from a Gender Perspective. A Guideline*. Netherlands Development Organisation (SNV), Holland.

144 (Goyder et al, 1998)

145 Johnson, S. (2000). 'Gender Impact Assessment in Microfinance and Microenterprise: Why and How'. *Development in Practice*, Vol. 10, No. 1, February 2000: 89-93.

146 Johansson, R. (2003). *Case Study Methodology*, p2. Available at: http://www.psyking.net/htmlobj-3839/case_study_methodology-_rolf_johansson_ver_2.pdf (Accessed 20 April 2019).

147 Stake, R. (1995). The Art of Case Study Research. Thousand Oaks, London, New Delhi: Sage; and Patton, M.Q. (1990). *Qualitative Evaluation and Research Methods* 2nd ed. Newbury Park, California: Sage Publications.

148 Denzin, N.K., & Lincoln, Y. (2003). Collecting and interpreting qualitative materials. Thousand Oaks, California: SAGE.

149 Domegan, C. & Fleming, D. (2007). *Marketing Research in Ireland, Theory and Practice*, 3rd edition. Dublin: Gill and MacMillan, p23.

150 Myers, D.G. (2009). 'Using new interactive media to enhance the teaching of psychology (and other disciplines) in developing countries'. *Perspectives on Psychological Science*. (4): 99-100.

151 Sprinthall, R.C., Schmutte, G.T. & Sirois, L. (1991). *Understanding Educational Research*. New Jersey: Prentice-Hall.

152 Denzin, N.K., & Lincoln, Y. (2003). Collecting and interpreting qualitative materials. Thousand Oaks, California: SAGE.

153 Hittleman, D.R., and Simon, A.J. (1997). *Interpreting Educational Research: An introduction for consumers of research* (2nd Ed.). Upper Saddle River, NJ: Prentice-Hall.

154 Painter, D. & Rigsby, L. (2005). *Data Analysis*. Available at: http://gse.gmu.edu/research/tr/TRanalysis.shtml. (Accessed 11 January 2019).

155 Ritchie, J. & Lewis. J. (eds.) (2003). *Qualitative Research Practice: A Guide for Social Science Students and Researchers*. Sage Publications, London.

156 Duneier, M (1999). *Slim's Table*. Chicago: University of Chicago Press.

157 Yin, R.K. (1989). *Case study research: Design and methods. Applied Social Research Series*. Vol. 5. London: Sage.

158 Creswell (2003).Effect of Service Quality and Marketing Stimuli on Customer Satisfaction: The Mediating Role of Purchasing Decisions Available at: http://www.sciepub.com/reference/159651 Accessed 12 April 2019.

159 Patton, M.Q. (1990). *Qualitative Evaluation and Research Methods* 2nd ed. Newbury Park, California: Sage Publications.

160 wikiHow. (2019). How to Do a Case Study. Adapted from: https://www.wikihow.com/Do-a-Case-Study (Accessed 20 April 2019).

161 wikiHow. (2019). How to Do a Case Study. Adapted from: https://www.wikihow.com/Do-a-Case-Study (Accessed 20 April 2019).

162 Murphy, L. (2018). *How to Write a Case Study in 2019 That Increases Conversions [+ Free Template]*. Adapted from: https://www.impactbnd.com/blog/case-study-template (Accessed 21 April 2019).

163 Gutu, O. (2018). *Gender mainstreaming in projects: a case study*. Available at: https://myprojectdelight.com/2018/07/25/gender-mainstreaming-in-projects-a-case-study/ (Accessed 22 April 2019).

164 QS Digital Marketing. (n.d.). The Five Best and Worst Attempts At Bridging The Gender Gap. Available at: https://www.qs.com/five-campaigns-that-tried-to-bridge-the-gender-gap/ (Accessed 29 April 2019).

165 QS Digital Marketing. (n.d.). The Five Best and Worst Attempts At Bridging The Gender Gap. Available at: https://www.qs.com/five-campaigns-that-tried-to-bridge-the-gender-gap/ (Accessed 29 April 2019).

166 Rose, C (2009) 12 Basic Guidelines for Campaign Strategy, Available at: http://www.campaignstrategy.org/articles/12basicguidelines.pdf (Accessed 11 April 2019).

167 Gender and Development Network. (2017). *Intersectionality: Reflections from the Gender & Development Network*. Available at: https://static1.squarespace.com/static/536c4ee8e4b0b60bc6ca7c74/t/5a130e9d53450a0abd9c0f8f/1511198367912/Intersectionality+GADN+thinkpiece+November+2017.pdf (Accessed 11 April 2019)

168 Gender and Development Network. (2017). *Intersectionality: Reflections from the Gender & Development Network*. Available at: https://static1.squarespace. com/static/536c4ee8e4b0b60bc6ca7c74/t/5a130e9d53450a0abd9c0f 8f/1511198367912/Intersectionality+GADN+thinkpiece+November+2017. pdf (Accessed 11 April 2019).

169 QS Digital Marketing. (n.d.). The Five Best and Worst Attempts At Bridging The Gender Gap. Available at: https://www.qs.com/five-campaigns-that-tried-to-bridge-the-gender-gap/ (Accessed 22 April 2019).

170 Mathebula, V. (2018). *Challenges that remain a hindrance in attaining gender equality in South Africa*. Available at: http://www.cge.org.za/challenges-that-remain-a-hindrance-in-attaining-gender-equality-in-south-africa/ Accessed 21 April 2019.

171 BI Norwegian Business School. *Empowering Gender Equality*. Adapted from: https://www.bi.edu/content/winter-is-coming/empowering-gender-equality/ (Accessed 21 April 2019).

172 BI Norwegian Business School. *Empowering Gender Equality*. Adapted from: https://www.bi.edu/content/winter-is-coming/empowering-gender-equality/ (Accessed 21 April 2019).

173 European Institute for Gender Equality. (n.d.). Institutional Transformation: What is institutional transformation. Available at: https://eige.europa.eu/ gender-mainstreaming/toolkits/gender-institutional-transformation/what-institutional-transformation Accessed: 10 April 2019.

174 Trachsel, H. (2014). Six ways to fix gender inequality at work. Available at: https://www.weforum.org/agenda/2014/10/six-ways-fix-gender-inequality-workplace/ (Accessed 19 April 2019).

175 Caprino, K. (2015). *6 Proven Strategies That Move The Needle On Gender Equality In Corporate America*. Adapted from: https://www.forbes.com/sites/ kathycaprino/2015/03/17/6-proven-strategies-that-move-the-needle-on-gender-equality-in-corporate-america/#5c93ec31fd64 (Accessed 18 April 2019).

176 Schwab, K. (2015). World Economic Forum: Preface. Available at: http://reports. weforum.org/global-gender-gap-report-2015/preface/ (Accessed 18 April 2019).

177 Workplace Gender Equality Agency. (2018). The business case. Available at: https://www.wgea.gov.au/topics/workplace-gender-equality/the-business-case (Accessed 18 April 2019).

178 Goldman Sachs & J.B. Were. (2009). Australia's hidden resource: the economic case for increasing female participation. Available at: http://www.asx.com.au/ documents/about/gsjbw_economic_case_for_increasing_female_par ticipation. pdf. (Accessed on 17 September 2018).

179 KPMG. (2018). *Improving workforce participation rates for women could boost GDP*. Available at: (https://home.kpmg/au/en/home/media/press-releases/2018/04/improving-workforce-participation-rates-for-woman-could-boost-gdp-26-april-2018.html (Accessed 19 April 2019).

180 Workplace Gender Equality Agency. (2018). The business case. Available at: https://www.wgea.gov.au/topics/workplace-gender-equality/the-business-case (Accessed 18 April 2019).

181 Russell, G. & O'Leary, J. (2012). *Men Get flexible! Mainstreaming Flexible work in Australian Business.* Sydney: Diversity Council Australia. Available at: https://xyonline.net/sites/xyonline.net/files/Russell%2C%20Men%20Get%20Flexible%202012.pdf. (Accessed 5 March 2019).

182 Workplace Gender Equality Agency. (2018). The business case. Available at: https://www.wgea.gov.au/topics/workplace-gender-equality/the-business-case (Accessed 18 April 2019).

183 Workplace Gender Equality Agency. (2018). The business case. Available at: https://www.wgea.gov.au/topics/workplace-gender-equality/the-business-case (Accessed 18 April 2019).

184 Noland, M., Moran, T., & Kotschwar, B.R. (2016). Is Gender Diversity Profitable? Evidence from a Global Survey. Peterson Institute for International Economics Working Paper, pp. 16-3.

185 Gratton, L, Kelan, E, Voigt, A, Walker, L and Wolfram H-J. (2007). Innovative Potential: Men and Women in Teams, Executive Summary; Credit Suisse (2012), Gender Diversity and Corporate Performance, Credit Suisse Research Institute.

186 Excite Education. (n.d.). Gender inequality in the Workplace. Available at: http://www.excite.com/education/blog/gender-inequality-in-the-workplace (Accessed 19 April 2019).

187 Excite Education. (n.d.). Gender inequality in the Workplace. Available at: http://www.excite.com/education/blog/gender-inequality-in-the-workplace (Accessed 20 April 2019).

188 Forensic Magazine. (2013). *Using Positive Reinforcement in Employee Motivation.* Available at: https://www.forensicmag.com/article/2013/09/using-positive-reinforcement-employee-motivation (Accessed 21 April 2019).

189 Forensic Magazine. (2013). *Using Positive Reinforcement in Employee Motivation.* Available at: https://www.forensicmag.com/article/2013/09/using-positive-reinforcement-employee-motivation (Accessed 22 April 2019).

190 Rebecca, M. (2012). *Positive Reinforcement in the Workplace.* Available at: https://trainingindustry.com/articles/leadership/positive-reinforcement-in-the-workplace/ (Accessed 24 April 2019).

Index

www.ingramcontent.com/pod-product-compliance
Lightning Source LLC
Chambersburg PA
CBHW072351200326
41519CB00015B/3736